SPORTS CAREER TRANSITION

TITLE

Sports Career Transition

by Dr Shane Gould

Bicheno, Tasmania
Australia 2024

Sports Career Transition

SHANE E GOULD

AUTHOR

Shane Gould

A vital guide for athletes and coaches to mentally and emotionally prepare for retirement and cope with adjusting to life after sport. With autobiographical experiences of Shane Gould world champion swimmer.

CONTENTS

Title - ii
Author - iv
Text Insert - v
How to use this book - xi

~ONE~

Introduction Begin Here
1

~TWO~

Cost of poor planning
11

~THREE~

Sports retirement is a transition
35

~FOUR~

Keep active, keep moving
45

~FIVE~

Helpers can hinder growth
51

~SIX~

Catching up on education

59

~SEVEN~

Real friends or 'YES' people?

67

~EIGHT~

Planning now while training

83

~NINE~

Preparations as you plan to retire

93

~TEN~

Memory 'banking'

99

~ELEVEN~

Gratitude and affirmations

103

About the Author - 113
Author Dr Shane Gould Australian sporting legend - 114
Suggested sources of help - 117
Acknowledgements - 118

Copyright © 2024 by Shane Gould

All rights reserved. No part of this book may be reproduced in any manner whatsoever without written permission except in the case of brief quotations embodied in critical articles and reviews.

First Printing November 2024

shanegouldswimming@gmail.com

Published by Shane Gould Enterprises P/L

PO Box 150 Bicheno, Tasmania AUSTRALIA

How to use this book

This book is a guide to understanding often confusing emotions and negative self-talk about retiring from sports to transition to life without the sport you love.

It may answer your questions or as intended, guide you to an action plan. If you or your loved ones think you need professional help like counselling, then please look into it.

There are questions and optional tasks to do as preparation to the process of leaving sport and beginning your new life. They are suggestions only that I and other athletes have found useful.

~ One ~

INTRODUCTION BEGIN HERE

Planning to retire or just retired?

Retiring from sport is a major life event. Anticipating it creates anxiety from the uncertainty of what lies ahead. When you stop playing sport, there is a lot to lose, which can make you sad. It takes work to adjust to cope with changes in your sport lifestyle. You will need to get used to not having your teammates around you. You will lose some of the privileges of being an athlete. You will probably miss the pleasure of being athletic, training and competing. It takes time and personal work to deal with the changes. It's worth the effort and you are worthy of supportive care.

I'm sure you've heard of some horror stories about high-profile athletes who had trouble coping with retirement. Some have been on self-destructive benders with alcohol, drugs or violence against a loved one. Not just those athletes who suffered from brain damaging, personality-altering concussions. It's known that concussion can cause behaviour changes. Grief from lack of processing the loss of sporting life can also cause behaviour changes. You don't want to be one of those people whose good athletic reputations are tarnished by unsociable behaviours.

Your behaviour after retiring may not be negative in the extreme but you will be emotionally and mentally affected by the changes as you adapt. You may feel relief from the burden of unrealised ambitions, or impossible goals but then feel guilty or ashamed. Another feeling is likely to be melancholy a nostalgia for missing your lifestyle, then possibly in some instances, leading to depression which will require medical help.

The good news is that you are not the only one who struggles with being a retired athlete. The bad news is that you will have to grapple with the switch. During the transition you will feel strange confusing emotions and might mentally question your self-worth and purpose. You will have to face the realities of living without the whole gamut of elements of your sporting life.

I can assure you, given some time, your life after sport will be interesting, fulfilling, challenging in the best ways, and enjoyable.

I have written this from my own experiences as the world's best female swimmer in the 1970's and lifelong Australian sporting legend. I am an inductee of the International Women's Sports Hall of Fame and Australian of the Year. I messed up my retirement, without debriefing from my swimming career when I was 17 years old. But I have since gone through the process of reconciling my achievements, identity and ordinary life through counselling and understanding the powerful dynamics of a sporting lifestyle.

I know that being an athlete provides many privileges, is a significant shaper of identity and a compelling way to demonstrate innate physicality. Leaving sport will therefore influence your sense of self, a purpose in life and ways to express being-in-the-world

This guide is for any sportsperson who has identified with being an athlete whether you are a 16-year-old girl who had to stop playing because you were bullied and shunned by mean girls on the team, or whether you found yourself a 'big fish' in a small pond and moved to a state or college team, shocked by being the 'little fish' in a big pond.

Retiring from sport is a process, not a hard end even though there will be the last game, the last race, the last training session. You will take from your sports life all of who you are and have experienced but apply yourself to life in a different way. You can still play informal sport and be active, but it's not the same. Changing to life without your main sport is a transition, moving from one way of living toward another. The changes can be unsettling with confusing emotions that appear to come out of nowhere to hijack your mood and self-confidence. It is understandable because you are losing a lot. Loss causes grief. You have had a relationship with your coaches, the fans, your supporters. Significantly you've had years of familiar confidence with your magnificent performing physical body. Your identity is tied up with being an athlete too. There's a lot about your self to come to terms with and your life to reorganise.

Despite external changes you are still you, with a love of moving, good networks, and amazing self-awareness from being athletic. Each of those relationships with your sport, your teammates and with yourself will alter, creating a sense of loss, like a bereavement.

If you have experienced someone precious to you dying and been to their funeral, you may recognise similar emotions from the time of immediate sadness to later really missing them. Some sports transition commentators say athletes die twice. I don't believe so. Retirement is a living loss not a death. Your sports career time has just expired but you haven't died. Even though you may feel lost 'on the other side' you will find your way with other living, breathing people to share your life with.

Preparing to retire or just retired?

If you haven't yet retired it's ok to feel hesitant to look beyond your sports career, because all futures are uncertain. Your coach might make it more difficult by questioning your present commitment if she knows you are thinking of quitting. Ask them to be sympathetic about your thoughts of your future. They might even have useful some advice.

If you have just retired, the days and years ahead of you are still worth the effort of planning for it. You can make your future something to look forward to, despite the uncertainty. This book is for coaches too, who may be guiding their student through retirement or for themselves as they retire. The book also helps support crews like friends and family without whom an athlete cannot conduct their life as a sportsperson.

You may not have retired willingly. Forced retirement is the most difficult way to have to quit a sport you love. That's tough. Accepting there is no other course of action after pleading and negotiations, analysis of performances and reviewing your motivation. The reality that you're off the team must be faced head-on.

The fate of adolescents quitting sport alerts me to a widespread issue of them dropping out. Managing their 'retirement' applies to them too. The reasons to quit involve some different circumstances than adults retiring. Children who are successful when they are 8-12 then move into tougher competition can be disillusioned by less success if success is the primary motivator. Instilling a love of the sport at the outset might encourage teenagers to remain with the sport longer. Winning and success are extrinsic motivators. Enjoying the sport for all of the pleasure of it is intrinsic motivation. Other reasons why adolescents drop out of sport is young people grow at varying rates so a 12-year-old boy could be biologically 10 or conversely biologically more like a 14 year old. Rather than racing in set age groups, maybe racing (when the sport is based on times) by time would produce an ethos of true competition. A parent and a child can be excited by early success but it doesn't mean success at a later age. As one commentator of youth sport Wayne Goldsmith says, there are no professional 10 year-olds. The limited life experience of a child will affect their recreation choices in their late teens if they have been promised future triumphs, without understanding the complex hurdles and luck involved. Therefore the type of goals set are a reason for teenagers dropping out of sport. Big goals set too far away in time such as an Olympics in 8 years' time, can feel insurmountable however inspirational. In those cases, achievable short term seasonal goals are required to provide satisfaction and a desire to remain in the sport.

To paraphrase the Beatles song "Will you still be swimming/running when you're 64, when you're old and grey?" is a perspective on reasons to develop sport skills when young. You can be active even as you grow older.

Whatever age, upon quitting or retirement, you're going to miss so many things you weren't even aware of that you took for granted, such as supporters doing things for you. Some of the pain you may feel can be alleviated by simply understanding what a sports career transition involves. Then, what to do about your unique circumstances that are happening around your time of retirement. That is the purpose of this book and my mission to help you get the hang of what's going on for you.

Who am I to guide you?

There is hope, good things to look forward to and past events to celebrate. I know because I've muddled through coming to terms with my life without all the amazing excitement and thrills that I experienced 50 years ago when I was the world's best female swimmer. I didn't properly 'debrief' from my career, leaving me feeling melancholic when I rummaged through my sports memorabilia or after I attended awards events as a guest. I had periods of time when I was a reluctant hero because of the burden of responsibility to be a role model. The burden too, of being treated as a one-dimensional human being, Shane Gould the swimmer holding world records in 6 different events and 5 individual Olympic medals at Munich 1972. I am so much more and can do other amazing things besides swimming fast, like train a horse, teach surfing, build a house, raise 4 children, public speaking and create visual stories.

I found I was smart too, atypical of what athletes were thought to be - brawn with a beautiful body not able to have brains too. I have a PhD in the Culture of Swimming in Australia and a Masters of Art examining swimming images in contemporary art. I was ahead of my time when I researched athlete career transitions in the 1990's before it was realised that too many retired athletes fall through the cracks, emotionally abandoned by their sports federations or teams. I brought the problem to the attention of officials, academics, and the public.

Years later, I feel attempts to mitigate difficult transitions to post sport life is inadequate. Resumes, job interviews and job training does not fill the needs of athletes nor explain the causes of problematic adjustments to life after sport. Only elite athletes are offered career transition services in Australia and only some elite athletes access services.

This book fills the gap of information and guidance that is not being provided by sports organisations. Coaches need educating too. Both athletes and their coaches at all levels of sport need to understand themselves in relation to a bigger picture of life-matters. A broader perspective of where sport fits in the whole lifespan of an athlete will help to make sense of the experiences sport provides, therefore make the transition process more significant and maybe even easier.

What you will learn ?

Here are a few things you will get out of *Sports Career Transitions* What you will learn is you will find the capacity to transition to your new life as I have.

Transition implies movement towards something else while keeping the context of what you are moving away from. **Chapter One** is this introduction. I use stories of my own experiences in each of the chapters providing examples that you might relate to. **Chapter Two** is a story about me, as an example of the cost of not preparing and planning for retirement. There are elements you may identify with. **Chapter Three** redefines retirement explaining it as a transition requiring adjustments. Adapting takes time so be patient and kind with yourself. **Chapter Four** emphasises how important it is to keep moving, remain active to fulfil your inherent talents that give you joy. **Chapter Five** outlines some taken-for-granted privileges you've had when people do things for you when you should be doing them yourself, so you can develop as an independent adult. **Chapter Six** is about education and training. How important it is to be a learner, to engage with different people away from your sport and experience some sense of ordinariness where you are not the centre of attention. In **Chapter Seven** you will begin to learn about support that you will need. But you need your street smarts of reading people to work out who are the 'yes' people and who are the 'truth tellers'. Filtering out these people in your life can be confronting. You will need support, the 'truth tellers. I emphasise 'don't try to tough it out on your own', make sure it's with the people who care about you. **Chapter Eight** is about setting up that support and **Chapter Nine** challenges you to prepare for retirement well before you play your last game or do your last race. In the early days you should be able to use the free and low-cost services your sport provides. If they don't provide what you need, ask them if they will. If not, there will be services and all sorts of help to guide you through the transformation that you must go through. Some possibilities are listed in the back. I recommend trying to answer the questions posed through the chapters, as they will change your mindset and help you to understand yourself as you evolve. You can't go back to the life you had before your experiences in sport. It's impossible because you are a different person now than when you began in sport. You are older for one thing, also changed, to an astute, worldly-wise person now. You can only go forwards, advance progressively eyes wide open with bold resolve. **Chapter Ten** and **Chapter Eleven** are about acknowledging your sports life with 'memory banks' and celebrations. Beware the trophy room. You don't want to be a living museum. It can obstruct your path into favourable but uncharted territory. What is good for you is Gratitude and Affirmations, which are healthy for your state of mind and for those precious human relationships you have.

What to look forward to

Once you have accepted the inevitability of looming retirement (or have already retired) you can imagine and design your way of life, your work, your play, how you use your time, but it requires some 'elbow grease' and groundwork. Never fear the planning and the hard work though. You're good at that already.

Knowing now that you're not alone with your emotional and mental adjustments, here are some things other athletes have told me they look forward to after they retire.

Some are challenges, some of them require solutions you will need help with.

- They want to use their spare time to do things they couldn't do when in sport.
- They want to feel physically good
- And want to look fit too
- They want to feel useful
- They want to still feel important
- They want camaraderie like they had in their sports community
- They miss the freebies and special treatment
- They like to tell their stories and what they learned from sport
- They look forward to healing their injuries and be pain-free.
- They are keen on getting into new challenges
- They have feelings of sadness and don't know why
- They are wanting to find their true calling
- They want to reclaim their creative spirit to put zest into their life
- They want to commit to lifelong learning to always have purpose
- They want more time to be mindful
- They want energy to immerse in nature like growing plants or caring for a pet
- They want quality time with friends

- They see retirement as an opportunity as a 'do-over' a second chance at life
- Other things you look forward to

Other athletes like myself have found a way through the process of transition. You will too. Get help if you need it to debrief. Making sense of your career is part of that preparation for post-sports life. You can look forward to your new future.

The better the plan, the more likely you are prepared with good solutions to find your place beyond sport. You can modify your plan along the way if needed. The least helpful frame of mind is wallowing in self-pity. If that turns to being stuck in procrastination it can turn to frustration or depression. Self-destructive behaviours might follow.

There are downsides if you don't do some reasonable preparation. One cost if you don't plan is that you may feel ongoing, unresolved, mysterious melancholy or nostalgia that turns up unexpectedly out of the blue like I used to, as the following story demonstrates.

~ Two ~

COST OF POOR PLANNING

The cost of poor preparation for inevitable retirement

Climbing the tall metal ladder to the 'junk room' to get some winter clothes and tax papers, I was faced with jumbled stacks of boxes. I sighed thinking to myself, it's time to restore order to the junk room once again. I had to bend over under the low part of the roof, an upstairs area partitioned off as a storage place. As a result, it was an awkward space to climb over and keep tidy. It was always a chore to store more stuff or find things. With four young children, their kindergarten paintings, school reports and out-grown clothes, all added to the number of items originally stored there neatly. I noticed it had a strong smell of dust and rats and old ink, hardly a respectable place for significant papers and my sports memorabilia, let alone a 4-year-olds first finger painting!

Constrained by the afternoon school bus timetable, I rummaged through boxes and worn-out suitcases to find the items I needed. The lid of one wooden tea chest had come loose and as I moved to put it back in place and bang the nails into the rim, a rat leapt out. Surprised, I inhaled the dusty rat smell as it nimbly scampered across the disorganised containers. Peering inside the tea chest, I saw it contained mostly trophies wrapped in newspaper, a distinguished home for a rat with ready-supplied nesting materials. Fortunately, the most important papers were secured in the large white suitcase with a faded Australian Olympic Team sticker on the lid. Just to be sure a rat hadn't chewed through the suitcase, I opened it to check for rat habitat by flicking through some folders, scrapbooks of newspaper clippings lovingly compiled by grandfather "Poppa" Reid. I came across a series of large beautiful black and white photos taken by Time Life photographers when I broke a world record in 1972. A familiar wave of nostalgia came over me, a type of sadness I couldn't make sense of. As I closed the uninhabited case, I heard my husband come inside from the horse yards for our afternoon cuppa together before 4 hungry children arrived home from school. He noted I appeared morose, subdued. 'Have you been looking at your old stuff again?' 'Yes, I have' I said quietly. 'You shouldn't do that; it makes you miserable for days.' Avoiding looking at my memorabilia was a typical strategy I used to manage my confusing emotions.

In that moment I decided to change my approach to the artefacts of my extremely successful sports career to reconcile them, put them into some sort of order in my life not just the physical space. I resolved to make sense of the remarkable things I had accomplished including the places I'd been to, the people I met. I needed to bring them to my then-current life and somehow find a context, a meaning for them in my adult life. That resolution then and there began a monumental change in my life circumstances and self-acceptance.

After my performances at the 1972 Munich Olympic Games, where I won 5 individual medals (3 gold, 1 silver, and 1 bronze), I retired from competitive swimming at 17. It surprised the sporting world, as they couldn't understand my decision to retire so young at the top of my game.

I always challenge interrogators with that idea of *retirement*. (Interrogation is what it felt like, requiring me to justify myself.)

I thought you could only retire when you were old or from a paid job. Retirement in my mind was a dead end. I knew I had plenty to look forward to, I just couldn't communicate that to the adults pestering me for justifications. It was unthinkable for me to stop so young and at the top of my career. One Italian newspaper thought I must be pregnant "What will mother Shane do" was one headline. I was not pregnant. I just didn't want to compete anymore, I had other things I wanted to. It was awkward to try to explain my motivations as I was only just able to decipher my way of looking at things to myself. As I tried with little success to explain my gut instincts I tried another tack, define terms like any good schoolgirl defining the words in an essay question.

Even though the sport was professional in one sense, in the monetary sense it was not. It's important to note that I was not a professional swimmer, there were no monetary prizes in the 1970's. I was an amateur. This meant that I did not earn any money from swimming. So how could I retire when I was not professional? Although I was exceptional at swimming, I received no prize money, endorsements, or appearance fees while I was a competitor. The amateurism rules were very strict at that time, and even receiving a voucher for a prize was a cause for concern. The rules for amateur athletes changed in 1984. I did not retire because there was no money in it, I retired for other reasons.

Usually, when someone retires, it's from a professional money-earning occupation. Professional means financial remuneration. Now you think I might be splitting hairs with these definitions, but I'm not. I think it is a form of 'due diligence' to analyse a word meaning. Of course, I did 'retire' in the common use of the word. But I will keep on with the analysis of the meaning of the words retire and professional.

Another reason for highlighting the term professional is that the issues of retirement raised in this book affect amateur athletes and lower-level club and district athletes too. Retiring and transitioning to a life without sport is not just a problem for top level or elite athletes. Heck, it even affects a child in junior sport who doesn't want to play anymore or is not good enough to be on next season's team.

Let's have a deeper look at the term 'retire'. Most athletes are still young when they end their sports careers. Retire has movement, it is not inactive. Transition has movement from one career to another. 'Transition' seems more precise to an athlete making a change. Retirement involves the time of transition and is being used more and more in sporting circles.

So, sports career transition is a better idea than the hard end of passive retirement. The term 'retire' might worry young athletes if they associate it with retiring at an old age. It can be difficult for them to envisage life beyond sports, especially if they only think of older people with walking sticks.

The process of moving away from sports towards a different life—the transition time—requires thoughtful planning with support. It's been identified among elite athletes that ending a sports career feels like a loss, akin to when someone dies. However, quite distinctively, sports retirement is not a bereavement death; it is a 'living loss', a non-death loss, like divorce or moving house. Retiring from work can also cause feelings of grief like a bereavement.

Retirement is an inevitable part of an athlete's life. For some, it can be a bitter pill, making the reality harder. Avoiding the inescapable fact doesn't help either. It has to be dealt with. It takes thoughtful planning as retirement is an ongoing procedure, a transition moving toward something else.

The follow-on from thinking that retirement is from a peak in life, means that the only way out is downwards. The only direction from the peak of a career is metaphorically 'down', a difficult concept for young people who have their entire adult lives ahead of them. One way to reframe the idea of the 'peak' of a life could be seen *not* as a single mountain. Life ahead is more like a range of mountains with valleys in between. There are many more 'life mountains' to climb, with hidden valleys and mysterious forests along the way to get lost in, learn from, and explore.

"Athlete Career Transition" is a wordier term than "retire," but it provides a more helpful and instructive description. It indicates there is a path for a way through. This book is a guidepost to that route to the unknown.

Despite its common usage, I will continue to use "retire" interchangeably but with a qualified meaning, such as "process" or "transition."

When I'm asked about my retirement, I like to correct people by provocatively saying, "I didn't retire, I just stopped swimming at a highly competitive level," to offer them an alternative perspective. If the listener is curious, it gives me an opportunity to explain the broader, more accurate meaning of retiring. This is still the way I prefer to describe it. I stopped competitive swimming, but I still swam in the ocean if I fell off my surfboard, swam in pools for exercise, and swam in hotel pools for relaxation. I continued to swim, but in different ways for varied reasons. I love body surfing and ocean swimming now for fitness and the bliss of being in wild nature.

Sports fans, journalists, and swimming insiders made a big fuss about me 'stopping swimming' because I was just 17 years old, had only been to one Olympics, and was still the world record holder in several events. The public and my coach believed I could do more. I did, too, but I was excited by other challenges and other ideas that overrode my interest in swimming fast.

Why people retire

People retire for different reasons. Injuries force them out of sport, they age out with younger players taking their place, or they may grow fatigued with the lifestyle and commitment that the sport demands. The majority of Australian Football League players are involuntarily retired. Only about 30% retire by choice. Injury seems to be a major problem in contact sports like football and in high-volume, repetitive-movement sports like rowing, swimming, and cycling. Injury is only one of the reasons for being involuntarily retired. A coach might want a different combination of players making an all-round player redundant. Responsibilities after the birth of a child might delay parent-athletes from returning to competition in time for selection and be overlooked for the following season.

Another reason people retire could be a lack of money - the need to get a better-paying job. There is a level of sport that can be attained that doesn't supply quite enough prize money or scholarship funds to live, pay coaches, pay rent and travel to events. The Aussie Athlete Fund started by champion beach volleyballer Nat Cook financially helps up and coming athletes to pay for the travel and living finances they need. Not everyone can get scholarships like that. One of my sons, Tom Innes was a pro surfer 15 years ago. He was on the world qualifying tour in the top 100 surfers. He was very good. He was photographed deep inside tubes, and one time on the cover of a surf magazine about to have a really bad wipe out in Hawaii. One of his jobs was a surfboard tester for experimental hollow boards for Salomon and a model for their clothing. Despite having good sponsors and employers that let him come and go from hospitality jobs, he couldn't get into that next level of income. After 10 years or more at a high level, he decided he needed to get training for another career, which he did in graphic design and copyrighting then electrical engineering. His decision was reinforced by a tooth infection that prevented him from competing at his best in Japan. It would have been his breakthrough event. But not to be. He continued to compete but not at the same expensive international level. I still love to watch his grace and power and his wave selection smarts as he catches and rides waves. He still loves surfing when he can. I admire the way he chose to retire from top level surfing with his dignity intact, satisfied with his results with a future planned.

Another reason to retire is when something new and interesting comes on the horizon. A new challenge or a mission that is more exciting or stimulating than continuing to play sport. That was my main reason to stop competitive swimming. I discovered philosophy, ethics, theology, and environmental and social issues that gripped my attention.

Some older narratives about why I retired are attributed to me as being shy of public attention. I am not shy. If I was, I would never have participated in Australian Survivor and win it in 2018. The reason why journalists thought I didn't like public attention was that I moved to the other side of Australia away from the main media centres of Sydney and Melbourne, Consequently I was relatively inaccessible to reporters and photographers and the offices of sports organisations. It was a full day travelling one way to interview me or for me to travel and have me present prizes. I was not shy I just lived remotely. I was very active in my local community, doing ordinary things like many women in country towns.

I retired to pursue new opportunities. It was a positive thing moving towards things not just away from sport. I love projects, and I like challenges. I decided to sign with the new swimsuit company Arena, a branch of Adidas. Mark Spitz was endorsing the male swimsuits while I signed in 1973 on my 17th birthday, fully aware that this contract meant that I could no longer compete in swimming. This finality helped me make the decision. I had an offer from Speedo Australia to continue training and stay involved in the sport, but I chose the Arena/Adidas option.

Since then, I've had to repeatedly explain why I retired from swimming soon after my remarkable performance at the Olympics. It's frustrating that the timing and method of my retirement, at times, overshadows my swimming achievements. I want to be remembered for my swimming accomplishments, not just my 'early' retirement. Making that decision to retire was a lonesome time, but my father who was still involved with me as a parent-advisor, saw the benefits and supported me. He saw the Arena contract as an opportunity for me to earn money, travel, and learn about marketing and sales as an Australian ambassador with an esteemed international company. I was convinced. I was keen to begin a new adventure, a new project in product endorsement. On the side I studied social and environmental problems and Christianity.

Another aspect of the public tension around my retirement originated because of the values my mother, Shirley, and I shared. At times, I couldn't explain the deeper, intuitive reasons for my choice to retire. The future was uncertain, but I was optimistic. My mother had I shared intrinsic values – doing things for meaning rather than external rewards. My swimming lifestyle was more to me than winning medals and breaking records.

In the introductory chapter of the book my mother wrote in 1972, "Swimming the Shane Gould Way." She said, "This book is about what swimming *means* to Shane." I re-read the book in 2024 and transcribed it to a digital format to be republished in 2024 with special comments. I was astonished by the sentiment which I had forgotten, 'what swimming *means* to Shane'.

The statement struck me as very characteristic of my remarkable mother, Shirley Gould (nee Reid 1928-2013). The significance of swimming to a swimmer in the sense of meaningfulness is not often discussed. It must have influenced how I thought about it, as it was likely framed by my mother, from whom I learned so much.

Parents have a significant influence on their children's attitudes. For me, the meaning of swimming was the pleasure of swimming itself, the joy of moving, and the satisfaction of being coached to improve. Trying to win is in there, but it is not the primary meaning of swimming for me. I'm glad I had parents who helped me to appreciate the bigger picture of the sport and my involvement with it. For many sportspersons, happiness has rested on winning a medal.

No matter what you have been told, one match, one race, one shot will not define who you are. My parents made sure I wasn't going to be defined as Shane the Swimming champion. Im grateful of their value-based encouragement of my swimming experience. It causes me to reflect on not so good sport-parenting styles.

There has been criticism of the "ugly parent syndrome," where parents are overly involved and aggressive about their child's participation in a recreational sport. A parent at a sports field acting in an unsportsmanlike way may be reliving their own athletic careers or they place too much emphasis on winning, not enough on playing the game. Fortunately, my parents, especially my mother, were not like this. They were supportive of me and were guided by intrinsic values, not by extrinsic rewards.

Working out the meaning of life is still the highest motivation for the ways I choose to live and is their legacy to me.

Families can't help but be affected by the committed, talented athlete. If a child is determined to dedicate themselves to train and compete given the opportunity, it would take more than a team of horses to stop them. A sports career and then retiring from sport has a profound effect on the family. Ron and Shirley Gould had to learn how to be parents of a famous daughter as they went, often facing media intrusions and sifting through countless invitations. I'm sure they made mistakes as they learned, but I knew they had my best interests at heart, managing my present (as contemporary managers do) while guiding me toward my future. My three sisters also had to endure being 'Shane Gould's sister' all the while being competent at various things themselves.

Like many fit, active athletes, I faced some challenges after I stopped training and competing, such as weight gain, feeling sluggish and despondent, and missing the excitement of competitions. Youth, grief, ignorance about sports retirement transition meant I didn't know what I would miss or anticipate what was lost. On top of it all, I didn't have a debriefing to assess and celebrate large chunks of my sports life. I delve into the importance of celebrations more in chapter 10.

Circumstances beyond control affected the way the Munich Olympic team members didn't receive the accolades they deserved when we returned home to Australia.

The unique event was the tragic massacre of 11 Israeli athletes and officials in the Olympic village. The Olympic games were nearly cancelled because of it. The tragedy delayed the debriefing from my swimming career (and other Australian representatives) for 17 to 20 years. Although the sad event did not affect my performance, it did affect my ability to celebrate my victories. Unlike in the past and more recent returning teams, the Munich team had no street parade celebrations.

My high school did have a parade though – they welcomed me and another gold medallist Gail Neall who also attended the school, with a rousing reception. Without the official parades I felt that I didn't have the opportunity to celebrate my achievements adequately, with the supportive Australian public. Carrying the Olympic flame in a relay of 7 great Australian women athletes on its final lap at the Sydney 2000 Olympic Stadium before the cauldron was lit, fulfilled some of the previously uncelebrated moments. It was affirmative recognition honouring the past, amalgamating it with the present. In my role jogging 200metres with the torch, I did a little horse canter skip of joy, content with my identity synthesised while revelling in the metaphorical and literal spotlight.

What happens to your sports identity?

Identity is something that is challenged during sports career transitions. You know yourself as an athlete. Others know you as an athlete. You are confident and secure in being an athlete. It's a label for sure, it's an identity, even though it's not all of who you are. Identity is a set of characteristics not just one. An athlete identity dominates your sense of self. Being an athlete is impressive. Other people can easily identify you as an athlete which may be detrimental when they don't acknowledge the more subtle aspects of who you are and what you can do. Not only others will see you as one-dimensional, but you might also see yourself as one-dimensional too, neglecting other dynamic and interesting attributes. When you are no longer being an athlete who are you?

I've always acknowledged being labelled a swimmer. From the age of 7, I was known as Shane, the swimmer, and this identity shaped my development, later amplified as Shane Gould, the champion swimmer. When I eventually stopped competing, I struggled to establish my identity outside the sphere of swimming culture. Despite embracing new roles, I felt a lingering sense of loss of identity by not correctly addressing the end of my public swimming persona and the associated lifestyle. This was a cost to me for not preparing for my life after sport. As I have said, it was exhausting to repeatedly explain to adults why I retired from swimming, as many failed to understand the non-swimming aspects of my life. The deeper, authentic parts of me.

It's difficult to compete with the influence of media and the tendency to label retired athletes into specific character types. Athletes are often pigeonholed, like characters in movies or books, which makes it challenging to break free from those categories. However, just as certain actors can effectively portray diverse characters, athletes must maintain authenticity in their relationships with sports teams, clubs, fans, and the media. You are who you are but there is a private side that needs protecting. Oversharing on social media or autobiography is ill advised. I recommend maintain some privacy. It's crucial to ensure that your portrayal in the media aligns with your true self. If you are a sensitive animal lover, it will not detract from your competitive postures on the sports field. You need to embrace the fullness of yourself; the sporting aspect is only part of who you are.

Soon after the incident in the cluttered storage room in my farmhouse and the subsequent conversation with my husband, I had a graphic dream about being chased by a lion. I like to try to interpret my dreams as I think they are my subconscious thoughts trying to make sense of events, unravelling them, bringing them to my consciousness. I knew that the lion represented something powerful something that wasn't going to let me ignore it. I think my recent readings of the Narnia stories to my children, where Aslan was depicted as a lion to be both feared and respected, might have influenced my dream.

I studied Jungian dream interpretations during my philosophy course in 1977 titled "Great Ideas," which focused on the prominent philosophical concepts in the Western world. The course supervisor required her students to keep a dream diary. So, 20 years later I was still familiar with the potential of analysing dreams. Given this background, when I had the vivid dream about being chased by a lion, I paid close attention to it!

In my dream, the lion eventually caught up to me because I stopped running away from it. I turned around and faced it. It stopped, looked at me with big, soft eyes and allowed me to embrace its furry neck. I felt calm, safe. The touch was strong and soft, reminiscent of my horse Lalinka's mane and neck. Upon waking up, I analysed the dream carefully. This is the way I interpreted it:

The lion represented the power of my life, my name, my experiences, and wisdom. Running away was an avoidance strategy. Some elements of imposter syndrome too. (The imposter syndrome is a behavioural health phenomenon described as self-doubt, doubting skills, intellect or doubting accomplishments, typical among high achieving individuals). I decided it was time to embrace the power of my swimming self rather than avoid it and being scared of its potency.

The end of a sports career can be scary. How do you know if you're anxious about retiring or if you are suffering from post-sport melancholy? The following stories and chapters will give you examples from my life and some others. You will be able to identify and name the feelings you are feeling, and why. Career transition marks an imminent identity change that can be nerve-racking when it begins. Who am I? Where do I fit? What am I going to with myself? The questions are important, the feelings are real. The transition out of sports disrupts your life in ways you don't expect such as your sports identity, which was created by the things you are good at. The funny word *discombobulate* is a totally appropriate description for the confusing state of mind and the disconcerting way you may feel. This is quite different from your usual confident self.

I've been explaining the varied reasons what causes people to retire. Ending a career in sport is easier if it's your choice. It's harder if it comes as a shock when it's not your choice.

Some common reasons include aging out, lower performance that leads to being dropped from the team, injuries are another significant reason for having to retire. There will always be a younger rookie player who overshadows the old talent. A player might decide it's their time to go, having or found a new, more stimulating interest. When it's your choice to retire, you might just figure that it's time to give someone else a go and get on with other things in your life.

Age is a significant factor in retirement. Youth often plays a crucial role in high-level performances. For example, in swimming, athletes can continue competing into their early 30s, especially in shorter distance races like the 50m and 100m, which demand strength and speed but less endurance. As athletes get older, they typically lose the ability to sustain high heart rates over longer distances, making it harder to compete in endurance-based events. As you get older you might become more cautious – from experience – and so take fewer risks in effort or game commitment. Good functional health becomes a higher value. Dodging impacts, avoiding repetitive strains, distributing daily energy expenditure differently with greater family responsibilities means you can't give yourself physically and emotionally with the same dedication. This leaves an opening for another generation of sportswomen.

Being replaced by younger talent can be challenging, causing you to question your legacy, age, and ability. This can lead to a decision to retire or to find ways to contribute value to the team in a different capacity. Mentoring young players, coaching juniors, and umpiring are some roles that I can think of.

Injuries are another difficult reason for retirement. They can be sudden, unexpected, and undesired, leading to lifelong debilitation, recurring injuries, and surgeries. Coping with injuries can affect an athlete's emotional well-being, causing grief over losing physical capacity and the joy of athletic performance. There is a double loss. Loss of the physical ability to play and loss of a place on the team.

Bullying, racism and shunning can become overwhelming to a young person in youth sport, forcing retirement from that sport. Australian footballer Adam Goodes endured racism that shaped his character and perspective of the value of sport. His positive legacy is now a legend in Australian sport.

Preparing for the inevitability of retirement can ease the potential devastation caused by sudden forced retirement. Seeking counselling, sharing experiences, and having caring support can help athletes make sense of unexpected situations. Support systems will help deal with unpredictable emotions even in a career-ending situation of choice. Anxiety stress can manifest in poor sleep, recurring infections, and irritableness with loved ones. Debriefing with a team psychologist, coaches you trust, and helpful teammates can help make sense of what's going on for you. There is no shame in having problems, or having a crisis, you are not crazy in the sense of being mentally unwell. Your state of mind can be altered, the obstacles managed, the predicaments solved. The reason for debriefing is to allow feelings to be expressed while working through the grief of losing something important to you.

Debriefing, counselling or just talking it out

I first thought of debriefing when I heard a news item on the radio when I lived on the farm. The Australian Prime Minister at the time, Bob Hawke, was taking some old-World War I soldiers to Gallipoli for an anniversary event. The soldiers were returning to the place where they had experienced traumatising events 60 years earlier. After returning home, they were to be provided with debriefing services. This compassionate care starkly contrasted with the lack of support for soldiers returning from war in the 1920s. It was a counselling service long overdue.

My mother, Shirley Gould, was a social worker who learned about 'talk therapy' in the 1950s for mental health patients in Sydney. The term counselling only came into common language in the 1960s. From that time, the role of the subconscious was better understood, and mental health was an important 'thing' alongside physical health. Therapists realised mental health could be affected by life experiences such as trauma, grief, and loneliness. Psychologists formed many different theories and therapies to treat patients. Telling their problems to a therapist helped them cope with and deal with what they couldn't deal with on their own.

Group conversation, telling stories and getting advice from the witch doctors and tribal wise ones is as ancient as language. Counsel from a therapist is more nuanced, as long as the counsellor understand the dynamics of sports career transitions. Shirley Gould was a natural wise-woman who later added to her gift, as a family therapist, specialising in grief counselling.

My mother was supportive of me when I wanted to retire to begin other challenges, remembering that her focus was on my wellbeing and meaningfulness of the activities I was doing. Despite her expertise, she didn't know the effects of retiring from sport. A pattern of problems in athletes was gradually noticed only from the 1980's and 1990's. Shirley only had some understanding of the emotions I felt, though. She had trouble identifying the difference between being headstrong, a teenage rebellion, and distress from the grief of losing the lifestyle I enjoyed. I had trouble identifying low mood and loneliness myself, let alone being able to share it with anyone. She didn't fully connect my swimming loss to ways I expressed subsequent grief. She recognised it much later when she edited my autobiography Tumble Turns in 1998 (out of print but soon to be available as an audio book in 2025).

Coming to terms with the experiences of sport and leaving it can take quite a while. Sporting life is a very significant time of life, with powerful body, mind and emotional demands creating deep visceral memories. You feel and keep memory in your physical cells. As well as brain memory.

'Getting over it' is not the point. Understanding it, appreciating it, making sense of it, and relating to the past from the present are the challenges.

The concept of debriefing I heard about on the radio offered to the Australian soldiers really struck a chord with me in relation to my sporting life. I also began to understand the profound effects that war had on soldiers. Both grandparents on my father's side nursed soldiers and ministered to them in Egypt during the First World War. I was at an age where I could appreciate the lives of older generations, but all four of my grandparents who all lived well into their 70's, were no longer alive. I missed opportunity to show my respect to them that I felt later in my life.

I noticed the resemblance of returned soldiers' need for debriefing, with the significant adjustments that retiring athletes also had to make for post-sport life. Circumstances are totally different, but the need to talk over the feelings is the same.

The emotions of grief have been identified with retirement from work and sport, in coaches too. I suspect family members will grieve as well. Maybe fans will be sad when their favourite player retires too. Grief counselling has evolved, and there is a greater understanding that grieving is a process with no set conclusion. The stages of grief identified by Elizabeth Kubler-Ross in the 1970's is not linear. Accepting a loss doesn't mean grief goes away. There's no need to feel ashamed or guilty if grief still raises its head years later. Athletes from all sports at different levels transitioning out of their sports careers go through similar grieving processes. Developing coping mechanisms for disappointments, rejection, and stress is a life skill. A Swiss career counsellor recently told me that she has observed in her work that the quality of someone's coping mechanisms determines their ability to adapt to change. Protecting a loved one from failure and disappointment is unhelpful.

What is essential in a career transition, is to *be prepared* for the changes in life. Anticipating the transition phase after the ending, before establishing another way of 'doing life', is a place of in-between, similar to a tadpole turning into a frog or a caterpillar turning into a moth.

Roger Federer said in a speech to graduating students at Columbia University that he had to let go of his tennis life, evolve, and continue to grow. Wise words from the great man. Serena Williams used the same idea of evolving and growing when she retired from tennis.

Returning to the story of learning about the potential of debriefing for myself, I decided to seek help from my local doctor, a General Practitioner. I asked the doctor to refer me to sports psychologist specialists for a debriefing process. I hoped this would help me address the confusing and melancholic feelings I experienced when reflecting on my past sports career, or rummaging through memorabilia.

What I thought would be a simple and quick process was a prolonged time of personal growth. It ended up being the final straw to end my marriage. I had no idea this would occur due to reconciling the parts or aspects of my life, Shane the swimmer and Shane the family farming woman. This is not supposed to be a side story about divorce. I had to mention it because of how serious the cost of not preparing for retirement can be. It was agonising, disruptive, shameful, and hurtful to all concerned. I still have some sadness because I value mutual love in the integrity of marriage.

The positive side however is that it also liberated me from the unresolved experiences related to my intense public attention and personal achievements as a national icon and world champion. By embracing my whole self, I gained the vigour of a lioness. I have been able to have yet another rewarding life contributing amongst other things to drowning prevention, teaching, and inspiring adults to improve their swimming, and developing programs with my second husband Milt Nelms for people who are scared of the water.

One of the most encouraging discoveries was coming to an understanding by reading academic papers and reports about other athletes who experienced stress upon retirement. This gave a name to my feelings, which was a relief. Sports psychologists described this syndrome as "Sports Retirement Stress," later terming it "Athlete Career Transition," which is a type of loss, most often accompanied by expressions of grief. I realised I wasn't alone when I read the articles sent to me by sports psychologist Bob Grove and Sandy Gordon at University of Western Australia, Perth.

An additional benefit of learning about sports career transitions was understanding flow states. A flow state can occur during times of singular attention to a task. Nothing else seems to matter and time seems like it stands still. Action and consciousness meld together, resulting in a feeling of joy. I realised one of my joys from swimming was frequently being in a flow state. Yet another intrinsic motivation for doing sport.

I realised that being in flow isn't exclusive to sport; it can be experienced through other highly focused activities like painting, singing, creating, or writing.

I experience 'time standing still' when I surf and ride my horse in harmony. Flow is transferable to many situations.

I wasn't the only one feeling unresolved sadness about missing my sports life. I was warned that feelings of grief can keep recurring, but the physical pleasure of flow states can be sought in other activities. These insights helped me embrace my identity and sport experiences.

One of the psychologists I consulted suggested that I create a list of life skills adding flow states to it. Alongside skills like baking bread, milking a cow, and making speeches, I added "getting to the airport on time" and "time management" to the list.

I recommend making a list of life skills. It's like an inventory of valuables, like a business stock take. Write it on paper, the skills seem more concrete when handwritten. Start making a list now of your qualities, aptitudes, talents, know-how. It's reassuring to see on paper how many other things you are capable of besides being a good athlete.

There is anecdotal and clinical evidence of widespread rates of depression in retired athletes. I am not the only retired athlete who has experienced grief, depressed mood, and melancholy. It can put you in a slump, unmotivated to exercise or eat well. Fortunately, I had good instincts to mostly take care of myself physically, and I found another physical activity that was challenging, exciting, and culturally appealing – surfboard riding. It involved being out in nature, learning new ways of using water, getting sunshine and making new friends. When I read about some athletes being so depressed that they committed suicide or became addicted to alcohol, I thought my issues were mild. However, one cannot compare the severity of responses to retirement. Your own experience is important whether comparatively mild or so severe you need anti-depressant medication. Seeking good counselling and reading excellent academic papers, as well as discussing the overall syndrome with psychologists, helped me to affirm my feelings and ways to deal with them specific to my situation and circumstances of retiring from the sport. They were unique and valid at the same time as being universal.

Once I had processed some of my issues, I asked my (ex) husband if he could support me and hold the space at home if I was physically or emotionally absent so I could focus on debriefing my sports career. He graciously agreed when I said, 'Please give me a year to work this out.'

The more I read and understood my and others' retirement experiences, the more I believed I was onto something important for other athletes too, not just myself. During a trip to the Australian eastern states (I lived in Western Australia) for a sports award dinner or Olympic fundraiser, I travelled to Brisbane where I had a referral to another sports psychologist. I also went to see my old 1972 swimming teammate Michael Wenden. I asked Michael to be available to me if I needed him after I had a counselling session with sports psychologist Dr Lynagh, the father of rugby great Michael Lynagh. My friend Michael Wenden picked me up from the airport and took me to my professional appointment with Dr. Lynagh, then drove me back to the airport. Discussing my experiences with Michael, he said his retirement experience was not stressful. This was reassuring for me to hear. Not every athlete who retires has a difficult time adjusting to life without sport. His life consisted of being with his wife and children, having a paid skilled job to go to, and not long after, he took up management of an aquatics centre in the Gold Coast, Queensland. He was around swimming people, and the culture, played squash to keep fit, and had a purposeful life caring for his family. I'm not sure at what stage of his retired-from-swimming life he began to be a volunteer administrator with the Australian Olympic movement, but he took on organisational and leadership responsibilities, as well as being honoured by carrying the Olympic flag in the opening ceremony of the 2000 Sydney Olympics.

Michael wisely and instinctively took care of his own debriefing and processing of his stellar swimming career. He won gold medals in the 100m and 200m freestyle in the Mexico City Olympics in 1968 and placed in the finals of the same events in Munich in 1972 (on limited training due to his family and work commitments).

Even though Michael didn't fully understand my struggles, he cared enough to support me. All the literature about grief counselling emphasises the importance of support for someone who has suffered loss.

A few years after the trip to Brisbane, where Michael was by my side for emotional support, I attended another sports awards function in Melbourne as a guest. The exact timing is a bit of a blur. The events of the dinner though are etched into my memory. Typically, athletes are interviewed for the audience's entertainment at sports awards or fundraising events. That night, when it was my turn to be interviewed, I took over the conversation to focus on the topic I wanted to discuss. Rather than rehashing my achievements, I attempted to convey sincere messages in my responses about what swimming meant to me.

During the interview, the old question of why I retired so young after just one Olympics came up. I found myself speaking passionately about the hidden issue of stress and depression among top-level athletes' post-careers. I was in a flow state, speaking articulately without notes. Unexpectedly, my impassioned speech received a standing ovation, even with heavyweights like the Australian prime minister, Paul Keating, present in the audience. It was a humbling and astonishing experience, affirming the importance of the message I was trying to convey about athlete career transition.

After the speeches, a postgraduate student approached me, seeking advice on choosing a research topic for her master's degree at Victoria University. She mentioned wanting to study sports retirement, but her supervisor had dismissed it as an insignificant subject. I firmly encouraged her to pursue it, and she did. This student was Deidre Anderson, who later developed the Athlete Career and Education (ACE) program at the Victorian Institute of Sport, which was later adopted by the Australian Institute of Sport in Canberra and in the UK. She became a spokesperson for athlete career transitions and guided some of Australia's best athletes during their retirement transition.

Deidre and I have stayed in touch over the years; she interviewed me for her master's degree and shared academic papers with me as the general understanding of career transitions grew. Nevertheless, the ACE programs evolved into more traditional career advice services, focusing on CV writing, biographies, job applications, interview techniques, and educational advice. While valuable, I believe these services neglect to address the underlying issues I've highlighted in this guide to athlete career transition. In response the growing recognition of problematic retirements, some national sports bodies in Australia now ensure that their athletes are better prepared for life after sports by requiring education alongside training and competing. Counselling services are offered by some sports bodies but only for the elite. Similar sophisticated programs exist in other countries like Canada and some services for USA college athletes. Retirement from sport is much better understood as a transition process. Why is there avoidance of dealing with the inevitability of retirement?

~ Three ~

SPORTS RETIREMENT IS A TRANSITION

Sports retirement is a transition to another career.

Athletes, coaches, and sports officials usually prioritise the immediate attention of the athlete—focusing solely on their performance and training, neglecting considerations for life beyond sports. They fear that diverting attention elsewhere could result in a decline in passion and performance. Athletes must plan for life after sports while still dedicating themselves to their current training and competition. Coaches must support that process. Changing the perspective on the looming end of a career from something to dread to something to look forward to, can make a significant difference in the transition process.

Career transition is a human life stage like puberty. Human development involves various life stages, from babyhood and toddling to socialising in kindergarten and becoming independent from parents. Teenage years can be tough, with acne, desire for independence, emotional ups and downs, and newfound sexual urges. These are all part of growing from a kid to an adult. Adult stages include starting a family, accumulating possessions, children leaving home, going through menopause, and facing retirement. These transitions can be smooth or tough. Researchers studying athlete transitions have drawn parallels to these life stages, helping normalise the process and alleviate the stigma of difficult retirements.

I remember the time when David Lavalee, a researcher from the University of Western Australia supervised by Dr Bob Grove, came to interview me for his PhD study. We sat in a popular café in my hometown Margaret River, Western Australia, and he asked very insightful questions about athlete retirement. I was able to share some lesser-discussed issues with him, and in return, he helped me frame the issues as a life stage transition from one career to another. It was a great perspective that put the process into a context that was already well understood in other situations. David is now a world expert on athlete career transition.

Life after sports can be something to look forward to, stimulating and filled with interesting events and people. It doesn't have to be uncertain if planned properly.

- Retirement provides the opportunity to do things that were not possible during training and competitions, such as being present at family celebrations, participating more in friends' lives, having long lunches with conversation, enjoying study, or diving into a work career.
- Retirement releases energy to learn new physical activities or to
- Master manual skills like woodworking, gardening, crafts, or renovating.

I must have had good instincts to do meaningful actions post sport, because I did many things mentioned in the above bullet points. I did not do them from conscious planning, and it was over a period of 30 years! I love learning, I enjoy being creative and like all athletes I love being physical. Some farming skills were learned from necessity such as milking a cow, stacking hay bales and digging holes in a straight line for fenceposts.

In the early years, after I stopped swimming competitively, I took up various physical activities, including surfing and basketball, using hand tools for building, shovelling manure for compost, and constructing fences on our small farm. I learned to use an axe to chop firewood and sew on an old-fashioned treadle sewing machine. Some of those skills dovetailed with my interest in culture and social history. I liked learning the old ways of living. It's hard work using a hand drill from a ladder, drilling into 40-year-old recycled jarrah hardwood! The roof framing of the house is still held together with broken off drill bits and nails! I learned that if you have the right tools you can fabricate many things in building construction.

Similarly, as a metaphor, if you have the right skills, you can construct a new life for yourself. I would never have believed I would learn the physical difficulty of farm work without machines and power tools. Then have the satisfaction of straight fences that safely contained animals, the contentment of harvesting eggs and vegetables from a fox and crow proof shed.

I even learned how to plough with someone else's big horses and a single furrow plough. Different straight lines to pool lanes but equal attention to responding to nature. Swimming to me, if it was needing a definition is an interaction with water, being responsive just like being sensitive to the lifeforce of a horse. I love the memories of walking behind the horses stepping in the furrow hearing the delightful sounds of chains clanking and soil cut open by the ploughshare, followed by the aroma of freshly turned earth. Two generous older gentlemen taught me. One of them was Cecil Noakes. When he ploughed land to plant potatoes as his occupation in the 1940's, it took a day to plough an acre, walking 12 miles in the process. It was marvellous to hang out with the old men and women and hear how they lived with fewer machines and less disposable income. Social history is more interesting to me than the political-economic-military histories. I heard about struggles in the depression years, overcoming disappointing crop harvests, and joy of close community ties.

My intellectual curiosity was stimulated too, post retirement. I read a lot and listened to the radio. I studied philosophy and environmental studies at university, becoming aware of the decline in biodiversity, overgrazing, erosion, deforestation, and climate change. My husband and I planted trees on our 100 acres which prevented erosion and reduced the effects of strong soil-drying winds. Our pasture grasses lasted two weeks longer each season with tree shelter belts. With our conviction in environmental values, we protested against tree harvesting in the forest adjacent to our land. We saved some big old trees as a result. They were the seed trees for the forest and homes for possums, birds, and lizards. Eventually the forest was declared a reserve then a national park. You can't estimate the sense of purposefulness we felt when accomplishing environmental goals. We acted locally by thinking globally – linking us with people in a world-wide environmental movement.

We had a gardening business in Margaret River before we had our own children and ran a youth group for teenage kids. Through that I met with schoolteachers. In turn they recruited me as a school swimming teacher – teaching occurred in the ocean as there was no pool in the town at that time. Teaching swimming was a good avenue to remain connected in a roundabout way to my swimming name and heritage. I also started a swim school in a private backyard pool during the summer as a small business, mostly helping children who struggled with swimming breathing and deep water in the ocean lessons.

Much later in the 2000s I participated in masters swimming for a few years, conducted lessons for adult swimming improvement, and engaged in recreational ocean swimming. As a boost to affirming my champion swimmer identity, I reconnected with the elite community through commercial involvement leading up to the Sydney 2000 Olympics. Continued bonds with my sport reduced separation distress from what was an important aspect of my life. Years later, melancholic feelings still arise from time to time, not from regret but from loss of pleasurable involvement in training, competing, and travel. Swimming in the ocean dissolves many of those emotions. I can connect with that identity Shane the swimmer, but also do the thing I really love and am good at, swim.

I've listed all of these things as an example of what a retiring athlete in transition might think of doing for their personalised career transition. Sporting life is a pretty special time, it's no wonder we can feel sad and miss it. Fellow athletes, we must understand that feelings of grief, sadness, and longing for what we had, or what could have been, are normal responses to leaving sports behind. It's important to recognise and validate these feelings as part of the transitioning-out-of-sports-process.

I keep repeating it - planning for life after sports can help make this transition smoother. Athletes are already skilled at planning, whether it's for the competition season or off-season training. These planning skills can be applied to life after sports, including time management and preparation for new experiences. Similarly, the thrill of competition and the attention from fans may be missed, but there are ways to find fulfilment in other activities, as I've described what I did as an example. I remain a competitive person. Racing a man paddling back out to the line-up after catching a wave was fun to see their shocked face as a 'chick' paddled past them. About 90% of surfing is paddling, only 10% is riding a wave. My swimming arms transferred to board paddling. Thrills from exertion and competition can accumulate from numerous small, exciting moments rather than gaining it from big game days or intense training sessions.

Another way of planning is to enthusiastically and creatively design the life you want with the things you anticipate. You can look forward to some of those things you couldn't do because of commitments to your sports team. Some presumed privileges of an athlete might surprise you that you also miss, such as cheering crowds, product samples and people doing things for you. I am still reluctant to buy a swimsuit for $60 when I used to get them for free!

What is not known as you undergo your career life stage is how you will respond to the transition process. Everyone's experience is different.

Inner reorientations take time, even if outer reorientations have occurred. Being knowledgeable about career transitions, as discussed in this book, can provide valuable insight into potential challenges and emotions that may arise. Being ready, even if what occurs hits you like a proverbial bus. Grief is one of those emotions that can sneak up on you.

Grief is usually associated with death, a bereavement. Grief can be felt from any loss, small or large, experienced as a non-death sorrow.

Grief resulting from the loss of a sporting career is comparable to other non-death losses, such as divorce, relocation, losing a valuable possession, or being unable to have children. These types of losses create ongoing uncertainty and require constant adjustment. Seeking professional counselling services for grief can be beneficial for grieving athletes, especially when their loss is viewed in the context of other non-finite losses. While a sports psychologist may not be the best equipped to handle a client athlete experiencing ongoing sorrow or depression, a grief counsellor may be better suited for the task.

Recapping: An athlete's transition to life after sports involves more than just creating a resume and learning interview skills to get a paying job. While these are useful, they are not sufficient. One benefit though of doing some work career planning is that you can eliminate what you DON'T want to do. Another benefit of career counselling is you can identify skills you can transfer to another work career. An athlete has many more skills that can be used to transfer to a new life, different work. An inventory of transferable lifeskills can bolster a sense of self confidence, rebuild faith in oneself - which may have been shattered by forced retirement.

There may be uncertainty about life after sports, but athletes can plan by setting small goals, learning new informal sports, and utilising their existing skills. They can also recognise and appreciate the 'soft' skills they have developed alongside their physical abilities and gameplay. It's important to remember that retirement is the beginning of a transition, not an end. I keep saying this because of its importance.

Other meanings of transition are change, transformation, development, growth, and a work in progress. That makes it sound compelling, things to look forward to even as you look back with nostalgia.

Some athletes may particularly miss the excitement of competitions, the energy of the crowd, and their team's camaraderie. Seasonal routines and weekly routines provide familiar certainty. Changing routines can make you feel unbalanced. Maybe set up new routines that match your usual training regime. Getting up early to run or swim before starting work or setting aside weekend time to play vigorously in the park with family or old mates might match your old sport patterns. Im just suggesting these things as they come to mind recalling what I did or what I know other athletes do.

Talking directly – you will have to experiment with what works for you and what fits in with your responsibilities! A proviso, I wouldn't want my ex-surfer husband to be going to the beach at 5 pm for a late surf if we had young children. Fulfill family responsibilities first!

Old routines can be comfortingly familiar, but they will have to be modified. Just think of the rhythm of a playing season. There are seasonal and weekly downtimes, but it might be more pronounced in life after sports. You might feel bored. Just check in with yourself that it might just be a lack of dopamine, those feel-good hormones. Be careful of false dopamine hits from using social media, and 'doom scrolling' videos. Seek healthier natural alternatives. Watching the stars, observing birds, taking a short walk around the garden hand in hand with a loved one are replacement sources of feeling good. This is the time you looked forward to by retiring, ordinary everyday stuff.

Look on the bright side of things, there is something comforting and settling in the ordinary. It's a time for reflection, connecting with other aspects of life, dreaming, and enjoying time with loved ones and pets.

The 'ordinary' life offers peace and appeal because it helps establish new patterns and stabilise you from the exhausting physical and emotional highs and lows that sports can bring. After a long competition season, sickness often follows. The immune system can only handle so much stimulation before stress hormones are depleted, making room for bacterial and viral infections to take hold. A good holiday with plenty of sleep can be restorative not only during competition but also post-retirement as part of the transition. However, a long holiday with lots of sleep is not where you want to stay. It's a phase you pass through to a more productive, engaged, active life that will become your new normal.

The saying "slow down and smell the roses" is good advice for anyone. When athletes are used to intense stimulation, they may miss out on the beauty of little things. I take pleasure in noticing little birds flitting about, snatching insects from the air, the vast variety of sea life I swim with, the quirks of horse behaviour, the smells of the forest after rain, and sharing meals with visitors.

Another suggestion to manage your transition is talk about your time in sport. Visitors with a sympathetic ear may be your opportunity to deconstruct your sports life by talking about what you enjoyed and what you missed. It's a conversation that can help you make sense of what happened to you. However, there is a danger in hogging the whole time with a monologue about yourself. It's better to find a counsellor or write it down than burden someone with a one-way conversation.

Being aware of what you say and positively self-conscious of your feelings is your aim in becoming emotionally mature. Not hiding or squashing the feelings though. Transitioning away from sports can be traumatic and leave you feeling sad, angry, wistful, and longing for past glory if you don't prepare for it properly – firstly by acknowledging yourself as a person with valid thoughts and feelings.

A final thought about retirement-as-transition is to plan to stay active.

This is a human beings natural state for expressing ourselves and making sense of our interactions with the world. Human beings are physical beings. Some human beings like athletes, are more physical than others. Of course, you don't need to engage in the same amount or even the same type of activity. You just need to do some sort of physical activity, for the sake of your body who loves to move. So, what are some alternative activities you can consider?

~ Four ~

KEEP ACTIVE, KEEP MOVING

You are a mover so keep moving

What other sports or activities do you like to play? Think about how you could join in with a different formal sport or one of the many informal sports available in your area. Until I started surfing, using my water know-how, I tried to keep fit by swimming laps. For a year I couldn't find fulfillment in swimming in a pool doing a one-hour work out a few times a week and doing some land exercises in my loungeroom. There didn't seem to be any purpose for doing the swimming. I was unfit so my lap times were discouraging too! It wasn't until I found another way to get a buzz from being in water, that I regained some fitness and improved my mood. I didn't realise how much I enjoyed being in waves at the beach until I started body surfing again and then learn to surf on a board with a new boyfriend. Surfing became my go-to physical and social 'buzz' and the ocean and beach was my intimate interaction with nature. Later in my 40's I took up ocean swimming when it became a popular activity in a social fitness group and doing optional mass participation events.

Horses and food gardening were later added to my connections with nature and being physical. Nothing like the sweet smell of forking over compost with strong back and arm muscles. Maybe the smell of sweat of a horse could beat that, after a wind-in-your-hair ride along forestry trails!

Fulfilling your fundamental way of being in the world – being a mover - will moderate many problems you may be faced with post-sport. Fortunately, there's a marvellous diversity of ways of moving to choose from. It doesn't have to be the sport you were good at, but something like it, or it could be your sport but at a different lower level of commitment. There are many physical challenges available to fulfil your need to move. Who hasn't tested themselves by taking two steps at a time up a flight of stairs or deliberately taken the airport stairs with a heavy bag instead of the elevator?

Consider informal sports. 'Informal' sports are becoming recognised as highly significant for policymakers. They count towards planning for council sports grounds, wellness metrics and attributing value to the activity when it is not formalised as a membership club. Activities included in informal sports are not just running or hiking, but games like pick-up basketball, or beach cricket, company lunchtime volleyball, casual regular swim groups and so on.

I've been playing pickleball for 6 months once a week. I enjoy whacking a ball with a small bat, keeping score and being playful in the process. I feel joy in moving and playing, plus I get a puff and use my body to move adeptly. I also mix with people I wouldn't normally spend time with. I learned to play tennis when I was young, so I can still hit a ball with a bat. I played tennis after school with friends when I was indecisively transitioning out of swimming sport. The moral support and inclusiveness I felt with them gave me valuable experience of what it might be like doing ordinary things, not being the star, laughing at my missed shots and losing points. I was still ok, intact as a person accepted by my school buddies. Playing pickleball gives me the same feeling. I am active, competitive and laugh a lot, but Im not committed to being there every week.

I have found joy in physical activities involving horses. Horses, like humans, are athletes; they are physically expressive. I love seeing them spontaneously gallop around a large paddock tail and mane flying, full of delight. Its infectious, I know how they might be feeling. An athlete is athletic because they move either vigorously like a racehorse or steadily like a strong cart horse. The key aspect of a horse, which is the same as human athletes, is that they need to be active using their physical capacities, not stuck in a confined space without a job to do. I love to train a horse and am rewarded with a mutually respectful understanding of their behaviour and my clumsy or sensitive responses. They are forgiving if treated with kindness respect and leadership. I can modify my exertion according to my mood and age and the horses state of mind. We are physical together. Horses are one of nature's gifts whether you ride them or handle them on the ground. They are a joy.

It might be easy for some people to choose a new physical activity, while others may find it less obvious. I knew an Australian football athlete who was not only skilled with a ball but also excelled at swimming. He was in transition from his senior football career, ageing out. I suggested that he might enjoy playing water polo in retirement, as it is physically demanding like football games, but in the water. This is just one example of how someone can transfer their skills from one sport to another without feeling pressured to continue in a sport they may no longer be suited for due to aging or injury.

A negative impact of not moving or not exercising post-sport is weight gain. Some sports require a large expenditure of calories. Food intake must keep up with the body's need for energy, leading to a pattern of large meals with high calorific content, such as carbohydrate-rich foods and mood-depressing alcoholic drinks. Additionally, poor food choices can make low moods worse when you're not getting the minerals and vitamins and good protein needed for optimal mind-body health. Unfortunately, an athlete who loves food will quickly put on weight if they don't modify their intake to match their energy expenditure post retirement. This is where knowing the rules and skills of another sport before retiring can help make the transition smoother. You can keep moving and reduce the potential for weight gain with a calorie adjustment too.

There's nothing worse for a top-level athlete than feeling uncomfortable in ill-fitting clothes, unfit or incompetent when playing an unfamiliar sport. Suppose the athlete is already feeling bad about themselves, missing the excitement of the game, isolated from their team's support, and not receiving the praise they are used to. In that case, they can spiral into a low mood and become confused about the mixed emotions they are dealing with.

Continuing to move is a sure way to prevent sinking into severe depression and feelings of low self-worth. Exercise is the best medicine. However, if a hopeless emotional state leads to persistent depression, then professional medical help should be sought immediately.

However, it can be challenging to seek help if you feel like you have been abandoned to your own devices and can't attribute the strange feelings to a normal response to loss during that reorientation to the life changes taking place. There are resources in the back of this book. If there is no listing in your country or city, google search 'grief counsellors' in your area.

There will be support for you if you can't get it from your usual support systems. Remember, there are ways to become unstuck. Start with a walk in nature or phone a friend to ask about their life.

~ Five ~

HELPERS CAN HINDER GROWTH

D on't be surprised if your support crew stop doing things for you now that you are no longer an athlete.

Once you commit to moving, especially in nature, we can turn our attention to some of the taken-for-granted aspects of being an athlete that are rarely considered. I am hoping that career counsellors will add my insights to their understanding as they help guide clients through change and grief.

Being a talented athlete is highly valued in most societies. Sports policies, families, and social cultures all aim to support and assist talented individuals in achieving their goals. These people and systems come together to provide aspiring athletes with the help and encouragement needed to lead a successful athletic life. If you are one of these people, once you no longer pursue these aspirations and work towards those goals, you will no longer require the same level of help.

It's beneficial for your transition process to understand that during your athletic career, you have become accustomed to expecting and receiving help as if it is your right. You have been socialised to believe you should be admired and respected, to be inherently deserving. Therefore, it's important to not be surprised if your support system begins to diminish once you are no longer an athlete. It may feel like you are being neglected, but it's not abandonment – just a natural adjustment for all the people in your sporting life. You don't want to be that spoiled child always given what they want, not required to keep trying, failing, and learning. A spoiled child is not required to earn rewards for good behaviour or effort.

Your support systems usually come from your family when you begin to excel at sports as you grow up. They go out of their way to help you get to training, to organise holidays and outings around your competition schedule. The family's food menus might adapt to your preferences, and finances be directed unequally to the aspiring athletes' uniform and equipment needs. Those behaviours unwittingly create the grounds for raising an adult with a heightened sense of entitlement. A 'you owe me' attitude.

Unfortunately, entitlement can stunt a person from growing into genuine self-confidence. Feeling a sense of deservingness can undermine your athletic career because you feel entitled to success, rather than earn it. It's a form of exceptionalism, where you feel you deserve more than other people.

Another form of exceptionalism can come from an injury or problem you have had to overcome – where you feel like your problem is unique. Throughout the 2000's there was a rise in the problem of swimmers having shoulder injuries from repetitive strain, sudden increase in training or poor technique. A pattern developed and the problem is now a medical condition called 'swimmers' shoulder.' Before the examples of the problem became obvious as a widespread issue among swimmers, the individuals affected thought they were unique. They expected special treatment and extra attention, fostering a feeling of being a special case. Yes, they needed rehabilitation and modified training. For those that didn't succumb to the attitude of being extra special with the scarred badge of a shoulder reconstruction, they were able to receive the gifts of imperfection - vulnerability and compassion for others.

A spoiled child and an entitled adult have had people around them doing things for them. I call it the "I'll do it for you" syndrome. When I was in full training my sisters would do some of my chores so I could catch up on sleep on Sunday morning, I still had to do my share of the dishes and walking the dog though.

I created a script for a short morality play about entitlement. It goes like this; There are four actors in two separate scenes, two male actors and two female actors preparing and eating breakfast before going to training. One male athlete is disabled, the other male is able-bodied but the viewer does not know who is who. The other female actors play the role as mother or the wife of the two male athletes. The first scene is a man packing a sports bag before sitting down at a kitchen bench to eat breakfast, mostly prepared by the female in the kitchen. He forgot a knife, but the woman said, 'I'll get it for you, you relax and let your digestion work properly before training'. He later drank all his juice, and again the woman said "I'll get more for you. I'll do it for you". Several other examples of the man being waited on by the helper always accompanied the idea of "I'll do it for you"

Meanwhile the second scene showed the other man going through the same motions with the female mother or wife in a similar kitchen, but they shared the food preparation and securing the forgotten items. It was still unclear which athlete was able-bodied and who was disabled.

The play directs the attention and judgement of the viewer to the first athlete having many things being done for them, deceiving the viewer that they were the disabled person. The scenes of the second person preparing and eating breakfast were designed to make that person appear as if they were a capable, able-bodied person. The reveal of course is a shock. The first actor is the able-bodied person being impaired by the 'I'll do it for you' female actor, rendering him immature and dependent. Producing an entitled human being.

I'll do it for you, is problematic for a successful, healthy career transition away from sport. A life in sport has its perks, such as being waited on, being doted on, helped in kind and thoughtfully generous ways by well-meaning helpers. I've heard of incidents common to young footballers who did not know how to bank a cheque (before electronic banking), respond to invitations, purchase nutritious food in a supermarket on a budget, pay bills on time or know how to operate a washing machine. They had not learned how to take care of themselves. Other people did it for them.

In some of the cases I heard about, particularly men's football, the club was only interested in the man-boys playing well in the seasonal games without requiring personal efficacy in everyday life. The players were like expendable racehorses in a trainers' stable. Effectively nurturing them to be socially incompetent men or women, quite unable to take care of themselves as an independent adult. Exploited as an instrument of the football culture with little concern for their ability to function-in-the-world. I'm sure this lack of maturity would be embarrassing to a player if their immaturity was 'found out' by a journalist or other close insider. Losing face can turn to shame with the realisation of incompetence in contrast with non-playing friends and colleagues the same age.

The 'I'll do it for you' ethic breeds entitlement, a dangerous condition for an ego already habituated to being special with the real and expected devotion of supporters.

Other examples of people doing things for you are simple things such as: 'I'll wash your muddy boots for you', ' or 'no I'll pay for this coffee' and something like, 'While you're sleeping, I'll fill up your car with fuel'. The list is endless, as are the ways to train an athlete to be as dependent as a child, while making the helper feel important.

If the same immature persons had some physical limitations, they still could do many things for themselves, including making bad decisions as well as good decisions, engaging in kind behaviours, or being arrogantly selfish.

Just repeating this in different ways causes me to become indignant about how well-meaning supporters unwittingly facilitate the emotional-social stunting of an athlete. It can be seen in overindulged children too. Unfortunately, there are athletes I have seen who believe they are special in themselves and deserving of doting support such as in the I'll do it for you examples I've given. There can be a fine line between self-confidence in just being, and self-confidence from entitled specialness.

The opposite to entitled could be the imposter syndrome. This is where you feel like you don't deserve your success or your accolades or your talent. Hayley Lewis a great Australian swimmer in the 1990's and mother of an Australian swimmer Kai, has said on social media that she still feels at times undeserving, because the attention seems out of proportion. Contrasting back to privilege, is the feelings of being special not for your physical prowess or unique personal features, but that you deserve it because of who you are. I have had enough experience in life since my privileged years to know about having to do the 'bog work' such as cleaning up mud, washing toilets and waking at night to a sick child. Each of those chores are realty checks cross referencing with deservedness from entitlement.

There are numerous signs of this affliction. One is an inability to listen to others' stories, always bringing the subject back to self. Another is a constant comparison with others, breeding insecurities.

Entitlement can be overcome with some counselling and personal work beginning with acknowledging it as a problem. If this applies to you, remembering struggles is useful, recalling how you got to be good, embracing struggle rather than being discouraged by temporary setbacks. Practise setting goals and recall the ways to achieve them rather than expecting to accomplish them without effort. Family members may also feel they are special because of the extraordinary commitments made to the athlete. The sense of deservedness such as jumping the queue at the coffee shop or the wait list for a doctor's appointment are symptoms.

It just occurred to me that the support crew of the retiring/retired athlete may also have their sense of purposeful worth disrupted. I can imagine a parent committing themselves for 10 years or more to their child's athletic opportunity with selflessness. Their life revolves around the training regimes of their child, adapting mealtimes, sleep needs, medical appointments, media interviews, sponsor responsibilities, and game days, let alone plain personal organisation such as bookkeeping, responding to fan mail, doing household chores, and listening to stories of other members of the family.

How do you push back on this sense of heightened entitlement?

Entitlement can be interrupted by the way parents manage the home environment of an athlete. Parenting needs to include expectations of ordinary everyday behaviours and training their child to be a functioning independent adult. Living in the present doing a fair share of chores. What if that supportive parent dedicating their priorities to their athlete-child's life is left without anything to do when the child leaves home to train in another city or go on an extended competition tour overseas? Just imagine how much time that those parents can recover to do other things, to fill their days with something else meaningful. Sports retirement doesn't just affect the person playing sport. Supporters need time to adapt too.

When children leave home, it is a common life-stage. Parents can suffer from the 'empty nest syndrome'. It's not really a medical syndrome but a common feeling of loss when a child becomes independent, leaves home, and creates their own private life. If that young person is an athlete with an I'll-do-it-for-you parent, then there is a double hit of loss of purpose.

Siblings can be caught up in the maelstrom of sport games, race events, training regimes, fame, and media attention too. It's no wonder some can become resentful of distorted attention and unequal family financial allocation toward one child in the family with the 'special needs' of an athlete.

My mother Shirley identified the parallel of an athlete's unique needs with a child in the family with medical or behavioural 'special needs'. Examples of a special needs child are one who has many hospital visits due to illness. They may be deemed special in the family by having the privilege of the biggest bedroom to fit mobility equipment in it or simply needs that demand the attention of a parent to keep them from hurting themselves. Marriage relationships can be threatened in the process of raising a special needs child. Sibling resentments can cause hard feelings too.

Attention to the important sporting needs of one person in the family detracts from the ordinary needs of everyone else.

These examples hopefully highlight the critical nature of understanding the hidden, unidentified dynamics of an athlete's life in a family and what must be considered when an athlete negotiates the transitional passage to life without intense sporting involvement. *I'll do it for you* is one of those least recognised, camouflaged dynamic between athletes in relationships to their helpers.

The next consideration for sports career transition is education.

Athletes dedicate themselves to their sport with admirable diligence. The same diligence can be transferred to education or skills training for the workforce. Catch-up training may be required, but it must be done by you the athlete. You can't pass off your education to someone else to 'do it for you' in this case!

~ Six ~

CATCHING UP ON EDUCATION

How far behind are you on your education and work skills training?

Balancing sports training and competition with completing high school or university education can be challenging. It's difficult to pursue a trade apprenticeship when frequent travel interrupts the practical training classes. While dedicated to sports, time passes quickly, and people your own age graduate, start higher education, or begin working. Consequently, falling behind in education is likely, compared to peers who are already gaining work experience and financial stability. On the other hand, you may have been receiving a high income as a player, with appearance fees and endorsements on top of it. Your expenditure will need to be reined in if you don't have that same supply.

Getting financial advice while you are still competing is advisable. I can't give you financial advice, but I can offer you a tip. Learn to save by banking something from each payday. Put $10 or more into a savings account. It develops the savings habit with a savings buffer for when your post-sport income changes.

A top-level athlete whether playing in a team or doing an individual sport will undertake numerous competitions on travel teams away from home in other states or countries. Cricket teams as an example, spend many months overseas, putting great strain on educational advancement and partner relationships. Training camps also remove team members from their home environment. The Australian swimming team spent several weeks in Thailand between the Olympic trials and the 2024 Paris Games themselves. They then went to Europe for a staging camp for 2 weeks to adjust to the French time zone before finally moving into the Olympic village. Eight weeks away from home is a substantial amount of time! And that is before all the interstate parades, commercial appointments, and school visits on their return.

If the athlete is still in high school or participating in a tertiary education program, they will miss many hours of lessons and assignments. How can an athlete who is also a student, keep up with their education when they are required to travel for competitions and are absent from school? One way is through online learning, a technology that was not available to athletes in earlier times before the personal computer and the internet. Another option is to split one-year courses over 2 or 3 years. Unfortunately, dropping out altogether is an undesirable choice. My Australian high school education was disrupted by going to California post Olympics. Fortunately, I caught up two years later at an adult education college. Travel can be a great education, but basic schooling needs the formal discipline of time and effort to write essays and do projects to test learning. Surveys on the life satisfaction of athletes who are not engaged in learning or work outside of their athletic responsibilities indicate evidence of boredom, and anxiety about the future.

Student athletes who are adept at managing their time efficiently, have the advantage of being able to allocate sufficient time for studying and reading, even amidst their busy schedules filled with sports commitments.

In USA the collegiate sports system is an opportunity to play and study. It ends at round 22-25 years of age though. In Australia, sports schools, university sports scholarships, and supportive employers may provide opportunities for student athletes to take time off for training and development. National sports organizations actively pursue partnerships with companies that can provide apprenticeships and work experience opportunities. These are good strategies with the care of the athlete in mind.

Years ago, there was a clear division between the idea of brains versus brawn. It was believed that a person with physical strength could not possess academic prowess as well. This binary way of thinking was prevalent, with many other ways of approaching the world in these black-and-white 'either-or' terms. However, when the 1983 book by Howard Gardner 'Frames of Mind' became widely read, it introduced the idea of *'Multiple Intelligences'*, it also challenged the brains-brawn belief. People in the real world, including athletes and academics, know that an athlete can be academically, musically, or emotionally intelligent in addition to their physical prowess. Similarly, academics and brainy individuals are included in possessing physical intelligence or other forms of intelligence. Another influential book that transformed the brains-versus-brawn belief was Daniel Goleman's 1995 book 'Emotional Intelligence which redefined what it means to be smart. This introduced the concept of EQ (emotional quotient rather than IQ measures), which is now used by psychologists, counsellors, and individuals themselves. Goleman (1995) recognized that scoring well on traditional intelligence assessments is not a good predictor of academic achievement, career success, leadership skills, or mental and physical wellbeing. Instead, knowing and managing our emotions improves our relationships, manages our impulses, and motivates us toward value-driven goals.

Accepting the concept of multiple intelligences coincided with the professionalisation of sports, many of which were previously amateur.

In the same era, there was also a trend of smaller companies sponsoring youth sports teams. Being well-spoken representatives was highly desirable. It became common to see a local team with the name of a town's bakery, plumbing business, or car dealership on the jerseys of kids' sport teams. Individual athletes as sponsored figures also emerged. Some companies made sure that their sponsored athlete could speak coherently, be well-groomed, and able to speak meaningfully at sponsor or sporting events. An athlete can be physically and academically smart at the same time. The cultures of different sports must help young athletes to develop intellectual capacities at the same time as physical development.

As the older generation of sports administrators retire with their outmoded ways of doing things, younger managers and coaches can bring a completely different perspective on what a player needs, to grow into a mature adult. The mature adult athlete can be pursuing studies in physics, carpentry, teaching, medicine, small business management – each field requiring intellectual abilities that athletes were once stereotyped as not having.

Computer software and the internet have transformed the way courses can be delivered and received. In the late 1970s, my father, Ron Gould, used his marketing management skills, refined in the travel and airline industries, to work with the University of New England in Armidale, NSW. He was part of a team that streamlined the production and delivery of correspondence learning. Laboriously, course materials were printed out and posted to students, who then completed the required work and posted assignments back. Depending on the course, there was usually at least one week of face-to-face learning, but most of it could be done in your own time and place. I also did some correspondence studies in 1977 through the University of Western Australia, and electronically in 2007 through University of Tasmania, so I know how the transition from all face-to-face classes to online courses began. I know their value for competition student-athletes.

The coach or sporting organization should not prevent an athlete from focusing on activities beyond the control of the coach and administrators. In fact, some athlete funding is contingent on them gaining work experience or pursuing studies. However, this requirement can be punitive if the athlete does not receive the necessary support to fulfil these funding conditions. An exam might need to take priority over a training session. Coach and athlete have to both value education more highly than a few missed training sessions.

In the early 2000s, I was closely associated with a top-level athlete who hadn't learned how to set up email on their new desktop computer. As a result, they missed important training program emails. They could use the internet to find information and read news, but they didn't know how to communicate using email. After retiring, they discreetly learned to use electronic communications. None of the athlete's managers or coaches thought to check whether this person had learned the new technologies; they presumed.

This experience made me realise that athletes can be treated as mere commodities. What this person particularly needed was a trusted truth-teller to check on their well-being. Someone who cared about their whole development, not just a transactional relationship.

Fortunately, 15 years later and with a new generation of communication technologies, learning and career education is more possible, while athletes still compete during their extensive sports careers.

The advantages of learning during an athletic career are numerous. Beyond the confines of their sport, they can explore other realms. Living in the transient bubble of sport enables a distorted perspective of the real world. It can be a shock emerging from the contrived world of sports. A benefit of learning in a class or workplace is being with a different group of people outside of sports while still being friends with familiar fellow athletes.

- Becoming educated means there is less catch-up to do post-sport.
- Learning new things can help an athlete become open-minded to improving their sportive skills.
- Being a learner develops empathy for other learners and therefore, become a better teacher if they go into coaching.
- Being a beginner helps to relearn Process. Life is full of processes.

Learning can be like crossing a bridge from incompetence to competence, which can be referred to as the 'silly bridge'. For high-level achievers, ego may prevent being exposed to the 'humiliation' of not knowing. However, to reach proficiency, a learner/beginner must cross the 'silly bridge' and move to the other side where they can say, 'Now I know.' By crossing the silly bridge multiple times, one can confidently embrace lifelong learning like I have for personal development and skills upgrades.

Being a learner, a beginner, or a seeker of knowledge can help build humility by being open to correction from people who genuinely care for them as a person and not just as a tool for a team or a source of profit.

I am sure there are other advantages of learning while being an athlete than I have listed here. What do you think?

One caution - Don't do a course because you think you should. Study is not a safety net. That's not the point. The purpose of studying is to develop yourself as a person. Pick something that matters to you and the life you want to lead. Do something that cultivates your curiosity and makes you excited about learning or creating.

Being a top-level athlete with extensive competition experience provides an opportunity to be good at 'reading people'. This is a type of intelligence. Younger players can have people reading smarts too. It is another unrecognised 'soft skill' that can be transferred to life. Even those competing in individual sports can interpret their competitors' body language, postures, and facial expressions. Swimming is considered an individual sport, but training is conducted in a group. Even without goggles I can 'read' the rhythms, the quality of the bubbles in the water, the proximity and energy of my training partners and competitors. This know-how helped me to read the body language and attitudes of players in the strategic game of Survivor. Some of the Survivor players who played team sports disparaged my place in a voting alliance because they thought I was individualistic in relation to the sport I excelled in for 7 years. Little did they know how many teams I had been on – family of 6, work projects, recreational ball games – or how smart I was at reading my competitors in and out of the water.

The ability to read people is very useful when trying to discern who your real friends are and who are the 'YES' people just appeasing egos by 'bootlicking'. How can you tell who is who?

~ Seven ~

REAL FRIENDS OR 'YES' PEOPLE?

Working out who your real friends are from the "YES" people.

What are YES people? These people *do not* have your best interests at heart. They are scared to point out character flaws, public presentation frailties, inconsiderate behaviours, and entitlement postures.

Real friends can be trusted to say things to you for your benefit because they care. It's these friends, or at least just one friend, that an athlete needs to feel safe with and to feel that they can trust people.

In the past, I had close friends at school and in my training squad who I felt comfortable with, because I knew they cared about me. They weren't overawed with my public persona. They could tease me in a friendly way, and I didn't take offense. However, when I lived in California, I didn't have people close enough who would tell me the truth, to be 'truth-tellers', the opposite of a YES person.

In the year following the 1972 Olympics, I spent 5 months attending high school in California, partly to give my family relief, partly to find respite from the invasion of my life by the media, and partly to have a life experience that my father enthusiastically encouraged. I also trained with a swim team, but the level of training was only about 60% of what I was used to with my coaches back in Sydney. As a result, I gained weight and lost fitness and race speed.

I have a funny incident to share about my time with the family hosting me in California relating to 'truth tellers'. Their housekeeper washed and dried my clothes in an electric dryer, which made them seem too small for me. I thought the dryer had caused my clothes to shrink and asked if I could air dry them outside instead. My hosts agreed on the condition that I hang them up myself. Despite air drying my clothes for a few weeks, they still felt tight. That's when I realized that I had gained weight, not that my clothes had shrunk. It was a wake-up call for me to address my overeating and under exercising, as no one had been direct enough to point it out to me.

After 5 months living with my host family in Los Altos, my parents travelled with all of my sisters to California to visit me. They came to watch me compete in a major swimming competition and go to Disneyland. We had to decide whether I should stay and finish another year of Californian high school or return to Australia.

After spending time with me and seeing my disappointing swimming results, and noticing changes in my body, they made the decision for me and said that I would be going back home. I did not want to. I liked my independent life. I had no choice. Reluctantly I agreed. They were looking out for my well-being and knew I needed better support to be a successful athlete and maintain my overall health.

As a 16-year-old, I was at a difficult age to make decisions about my independence, and I didn't take their decisions well. I had a comfortable life in the US—I was allowed to use one of the family's cars, got my driver's license early, received a stipend, and had a relatively easy training schedule. School subjects were easy, and the ethics and philosophy courses were fascinating.

Reluctantly, I agreed to return to Australia with my family, but I was apprehensive about what kind of life awaited me after experiencing so much freedom and independence. Unfortunately, the shame of returning home unfit was compounded by having to withdraw from the first World Swimming Championships. Full blown rebellious teenage behaviour culminated in me 'running away from home' by train for 24 hours with $30 in my purse! I was planning to live on the beach near Byron Bay. Funny to think of now but it was a cry for help and the need for change.

I got as far as Armidale where I 'surrendered' to my mother who was there looking for a house to buy. I was able to negotiate with my parents a school and living situation where I still had some independence, while under some structured authority.

My key point is that well-known athletes, especially, require genuine relationships, not just transactional ones. My parents genuinely cared for me. A transactional relationship is one where each person does things for the other, expecting something in return. It's a give-and-take scenario with a bit of quid pro quo. Each person is willing to help the other if the favour is reciprocated immediately or at some point down the line. A sponsorship relationship is an example. However, a transactional relationship can become toxic if the favours are not reciprocated or if the other person only gets in touch with you when they need something.

During formative years, it takes time to learn who to trust and who to be cautious of. Being famous or a local hero during those years adds complexity to the natural teenage development of figuring out who will support you, who you can confide in, and who is trustworthy. It's important to nurture instincts to discern these things.

Two more incidents taught me who not to trust and what situations to potentially avoid. A year later in 1974 I was in France with Arena the new international swimwear brand born from Adidas. Still young, 17 I had left high school as I was too far behind (the following year I did adult education to finish the last two years of high school in one year), naive but cocky with self-confidence in my independence, living in a flat with my sister, having my own money and car and a job as a brand ambassador.

The naivety extended to the European fashion industry. Sports clothing was rapidly becoming fashion. The Arena executives managing my visit and promotions of the new Arena brand in Europe connected me with the significant Cacharel Brand to dress me while I attended launches, media appearances and product placements. They were beautiful clothes, smart casual, colourful patterns, and stylish designs. A big problem was my size. I was still overweight, so my trousers were tight, my bust caused buttons to spread, and I felt uncomfortable in my body. I was able to fake my roles enough to do the tasks I was asked but no one cared for me enough to talk to me on a 'real' level, to help me understand the fashion industry, direct me to some lifestyle exercise and dietary restraint, or supply me with larger, better fitting clothes!

My instincts were aroused about identifying people who cared and others who just objectified me.

I had another experience of objectification later that year, when I attended a swimwear promotion at a shopping centre in Wollongong, south of Sydney. After poor communication with the two people I travelled with, I was left at the service entry side of the shopping centre in the hot sun without a drink, after the shops had closed. My ride, who was my new boyfriend and his surfing mate, had gone surfing while I was at the shopping centre. We had planned to meet at a specific time and then go back to the beach so I could also go surfing. At that time, I was really into surfing, which was my new aquatic challenge and thrill. This following incident happened before the era of mobile phones.

I sat there in the sun for what felt like an eternity, with some boxes of samples. I didn't dare leave them to search for a shady spot or a shop to buy water. After nearly two hours of waiting, I was on the verge of tears from frustration and an overwhelming sense of loneliness that I had never experienced before. Even when the guys returned, they seemed oblivious to my situation and the impact of their delay in returning at the agreed time. I had difficulty identifying my feelings so I couldn't explain my despair. The surf was good, which seemed to be more important to them than collecting me. I'm sure they presumed the shops were still open and I was still doing the product promotions. I felt abandoned and uncared for.

That pivotal incident led my boyfriend (later my husband) to view advertising as evil, attributing it to my fame from competition, which he later equated to the root of war. His strong opinions and unconventional interpretations of my life and the world of elite sports, with which he had no experience, led to a flawed interpretation and misunderstanding. This became a significant issue that ultimately created irreconcilable differences in our perspectives. Despite once being on the same platform of attitudes towards over-consumption, we ended up with completely opposing views and the marriage ended.

The shopping centre affair created a fracture in both our lives before we even got married. I just wanted him to pick me up on time and take me surfing, but instead, he gave me a lecture about the downsides of competition and commerce. These were topics I was thinking about from philosophical perspectives of the role of transnational corporations and advertising in the negatives of globalisation but hadn't concluded an opinion at the time. (Wealth centralisation, cultural homogeneity and exploitation of labour and resources are some negatives of globalisation.)

This is a lengthy narrative from my personal experiences, reflecting my naivety about identifying true friends. Many years later, I can forgive my boyfriend/ex-husband, as well as the sporting officials and sponsor executives, for their lack of concern for my well-being. They were simply unaware of my needs and didn't grasp the complexities of an athlete undergoing career transition. Those adults did not know about how an athletes' identity and relationships are shaped during the competitive phase of an athlete's life.

My immature perspectives of athletes needs and the role of advertising in sport have since been straightened out with a mature understanding presented here from a wise standpoint. The issue of globalisation, politics and commerce in sport mega-events like Olympic games is another subject I covered in my PhD. I won't go into it here as it is a distraction from the subject at hand, the process of athletes transitioning away from sport.

Just as it is inevitable that an athlete will retire, it is inevitable that a new champion will emerge. Accepting a new champion coming after you, a new "It girl", is another aspect of figuring out who to trust while building self-confidence in other areas outside of sports. At some point, my mother shared a poem that helped me understand my experiences of being pushed aside, made redundant, and making room for the new up-and-coming champion.

The poem is "To an Athlete Dying Young" by A.E. Housman.

The poem reflects on a champion athlete who was once paraded in his hometown, celebrated for his achievements, and enthusiastically cheered by fans. However, while still in his prime, he died. He was brought back home to be buried without having to endure fading glory. The poem also addresses other themes, such as the idea that death is a release, youth and life are brief, and pessimistically, that human beings cannot count on earthly happiness or immortality. It's quite a grim message!

The line I remember as a good lesson is that fame is fleeting, and fans are fickle. There will always be a new champion, and fans will switch their doting loyalty to the next favourite.

To an Athlete Dying Young by AE Houseman
The time you won your town the race
We chaired you through the marketplace;
Man and boy stood cheering by,
And home we brought you shoulder-high.

Today, the road all runners come,
Shoulder-high we bring you home,
And set you at your threshold down,
Townsman of a stiller town.

Smart lad, to slip betimes away
From fields where glory does not stay,
And early though the laurel grows
It withers quicker than the rose.

Eyes the shady night has shut
Cannot see the record cut,
And silence sounds no worse than cheers
After earth has stopped the ears.

Now you will not swell the rout
Of lads that wore their honours out,
Runners whom renown outran
And the name died before the man.

So set, before its echoes fade,
The fleet foot on the sill of shade,
And hold to the low lintel up
The still-defended challenge-cup.

And round that early-laurelled head
Will flock to gaze the strengthless dead,
And find unwithered on its curls
The garland briefer than a girl's.

Let's look at another poet who also has a way with words about fame,
Fame is a fickle food by Emily Dickinson, written in 1659.

Fame is a fickle food
Upon a shifting plate
Whose table once a
Guest but not
The second time is set.

Whose crumbs the crows inspect
And with ironic caw
Flap past it to the
Farmer's Corn—
Men eat of it and die.

There is a lot in the meaning of Emily Dickinson's poem but what I take from it is the issue of fame and its fleeting nature. Is it worth it? Who can you trust?

Some commentators find her poem cryptic but believe it speaks volumes about the transience and instability of our desires and ambitions, including fame. It's worth noting that moral character was a dominant theme in the post-reformation church eras, which shines through in the poem.

I have spent a lifetime grappling with my fame. Emily Dickinson's poem raises complex issues about fame that I have pondered deeply.

Vanity can be elevated by fame, a self-serving sin according to some moral philosophies including the Christian bible.

Elusiveness – fame is hard to attain because it relies on other people to recognise your accomplishments as something 'famous'. It is better to aim for being good at what you do rather than aim for fame which may occur because of being a very good athlete. Aiming for fame is elusive.

The cost of fame may be too high at a price that is not always worth paying. Costs may be personal and financial. Professional sports at just the right level can be financially lucrative though in the 21st C but not until a high level is reached. There are plenty of stories of aspiring athletes unable to afford a place to live or pay for nutritious food as they climb their way up the competitive ladder. The personal costs may be deteriorating relationships if players are away from home to train and compete, leaving siblings, spouses and children behind.

The obsessiveness of top-level sport at the level of being famous requires intense application to the point of an all-consuming passion ultimately being destructive because of the obsession. An insatiable hunger, always looking for the next big thing, can result in disappointment, a yearning unable to be satisfied. Hence the warning of the obsessive pursuit of fame.

This still rings true nearly 400 years after Dickinson wrote her poem. Being famous, even for a few years or a season, tests one's moral character and ethical values. In the 21st century, there are advantages to fame for some. Some who can leverage their reputations and notoriety beyond being an influencer can do a lot of good if they are positive role models.

Be careful what you wish for though! Being famous has its benefits, but there are also warnings. I have already stated more of those cautions—an athlete will have to retire at some stage to a less spectacular life and ask as I did, 'Was it worth it?' 'What just happened to me?!'

Another perspective I have of fame is being seen as *chosen*, singled out. The Chosen One theme is prevalent in fiction and in sport. It is an archetype, a model of an ideal person, that taps into a human desire for meaning and purpose while having a leader to follow. The idea that an individual is "special" and destined for great things can be psychologically compelling for sports writers and fans. It gives the hero's journey a sense of higher significance and inevitability.

Interesting to me is that quickly after a heroic athletic performance, a role model emerges by magic out of the fog of notoriety. I explain later why I have reservations about how athletes can be transmogrified to be a role model just by performing physically well. It's a huge demand on the young person, especially when the responsibility is not accompanied by training about how to act and behave as a role model. Champion Olympians like myself play expected roles for example as international diplomat, without training or much briefing. The expectation is irresponsible. Diplomacy is extremely important in world peace and human cooperation. Presuming that a newly fledged successful athlete, a 'chosen one' has the innate abilities as a world peace envoy is naïve. Soft diplomacy is a new concept in international relations.

Sport is frequently used for those political relationships. I just read in October 2024 that Papua New Guinea (PNG) want to form a Rugby League team and join the Australian NRL league. The Australian International relations minister said they would give PNG

$600 million to create aa new NRL team on the condition that PNG do not sign a security deal with China in their region. The minister admitted that Rugby League was part of the Australian Governments 'soft diplomacy'. I wonder if the players will know of those circumstances before they are recruited and their responsibility to fulfill the political goals.?

The Chosen One Archetype provides a clear storyline. It validates a good tale, such as athletic heroism. Sport role models are a type of chosen one with a heroic destiny. When the main character has a predetermined future it allows the author to guide the sports story towards a climactic conclusion where the hero fulfils their destined role. The rise of a new champion and their ongoing triumphs and tragedies is a satisfying cohesive storytelling experience. A Chosen One character who becomes a role model is a powerful storytelling tool recited by journalists and sports enthusiasts. We see that in the elevation of superb athletes known around the world such as Roger Federer, Serena Williams, Tiger Woods, Surfer Kelly Slater, and swimmer Michael Phelps. The GOAT (Greatest of all time) is a new name for these even more special chosen-ones. Having lived with animal goats, it's a great metaphor. Goats are resilient, strong minded, hardy, athletic, and can be great pets.

According to this discussion, beyond aiming to be a winner, an athlete's destiny may be to become a role model, attaining some sort of moral ascendance. The celebrated ancient Greek athletes were regarded as favoured by gods and, in some cases, traced back as descended from gods. Greek sports cannot be separated from Greek religion, and the ancient Olympics were a religious festival. The role model concept may be related to this tradition, but there is a modern take on it too. As I've said I think it is most peculiar that when an athlete succeeds; they automatically become a role mode. A person with unique talent who is transformed is expected to inspire, young people by their example and influence to participate in sport and aspire to sporting success.

As we know, there can be positive and negative role models. An undesirable role model undermines the idea of moral primacy attributed to all role models. Fallen stars are terribly disappointing.

If an athlete's destiny is to be a role model, something encouraged by sports cultures, does an athlete role model really help entice sport participation? Research says that only some young people begin to play sport because of observing a role model. Surveys show that parents and friends are more influential. What does inspire or encourage a child to take up a sport? How much incentive is intrinsic and how much is extrinsically motivated?

How much realism is described in the pitch to participate in sport?

The USA Olympic Training Centre in Colorado Springs has a saying: "Dream-believe-achieve" written in big letters above the entrance doors. This motto does not emphasise the realism. That is; achieving sport dreams requires hard work, dedication, teamwork, receive guidance from coaches, manage pressure, handle success and failure, and, most importantly, enjoying the sport.

It's as though success will result automatically, that being a winner is everyone's right, and a medal will bring happiness.

Benjamin Franklin, a prominent 'founding father' of the USA in the mid-1700s, is famously quoted as saying, "You can do anything you set your mind to." Adages like that were commonly used in folk society as a wise saying. Three hundred years later, it has been corrupted. Athletes use it in interviews as an inspirational saying, demonstrating their wisdom as a role model, or as a concluding aspirational remark. It is overused and has become a barrier to more thoughtful remarks that could help young people engage with sports with their "eyes wide open." It's easier to say that you have an Olympic dream inspired by a saying, than to put in the necessary work to achieve it. Selling a dream in this manner will disappoint an aspiring athlete and probably cause them to quit.

According to a survey in Australia, only 10% of elite athletes report that other elite athletes inspired them to start playing their current sport, while 59% were encouraged by parents and 29% by friends. The conclusion is that role models are less influential than parents. Despite this, most countries' sports policies focus on increasing participation by grooming elite athletes (as role models) to attract young children to sports.

Researchers found it hard to establish a cause-and-effect relationship between elite sports and widespread participation. Some studies suggest that elite athletes mainly inspire young people who are *already* involved and successful in a sport.

A major television event like a grand final or an Olympics might motivate a child to try a sport, but they will need support from parents and friends to keep at it. If you can recall why you took up your sport it might help the transition process out of sport. Did you play because you loved being on a team? Did you like getting attention? Do you continue to play because you liked getting a hot dog at the end of the game? Did you like doing the skills required of the sport? Did you have to play because all of your siblings were? Were they intrinsic or extrinsic reasons?

Did you expect success because you trusted in promises of the dream-believe-goal? If expected success hasn't occurred as assumed, then retirement will most likely incur disappointment, anger and self-doubt. Family support crews may also feel betrayed by false promises.

Family members are an integral part of an athlete's life. It's no surprise that they will also be affected by a retiring player. Unfortunately, unsatisfactory family relationships can increase tension in the home especially if the way parents relate to their sports prodigy are inappropriate during the years of playing and competing. One inappropriate way of relating is being a fan. Athletes need their parents to behave as a parent, not a fan or an agent.

When I mentioned *inappropriate* relationships it's in the sense of 'right relationships' detailed in the following example. If your brother or mother becomes your fan by saying "I'm your biggest fan," then the normal relationship of brother to brother or mother to son becomes distorted, effectively rupturing family ties. An athlete with special talent needs genuine, real relationships to keep a grip on reality - to which they will eventually have to return.

I can give an example of my own life about 'right relationships'.

My grandfather, "Poppa," was very proud of me, as evidenced by the beautifully collated newspaper cuttings he glued into scrapbooks I mentioned in my introductory story about the 'junk room'. Grandpa Clive Reid was a sociable person, very good shoe salesman and had an infectious laugh of delight. He was very particular about quality, good fitting shoes. I liked him. He belonged to a lawn bowls club and shared a beautiful garden nurtured by my grandma, Narnie, situated on the edge of a lake near a popular surfing beach north of Sydney. My family drove from Sydney to visit them regularly where Narnie and Poppa were happily retired. Once the brief hugs and welcome rituals concluded, Poppa brought out the scrapbooks he had updated in the last month. Sadly, I was rather insensitive to his pride and his labour. I pestered him to go to his room under the house where he had his model trains set up. I wanted to spend time with him and do things Grandpa and granddaughter could enjoy together. I didn't mind him inspecting my shoes when I saw him, but I didn't want Poppa to be my fan.

I wish I had better clarity on this at the time, as he was a lovely man, and I don't feel like I showed the right amount of appreciation for his time and effort in recording my sports career from the media. I still have those scrapbooks. They probably need to be digitised, but I keep them as they are, as I remember my grandpa and his handiwork, with the sound of electric model trains in the background.

My grandmother, Narnie, was less impressed with my fame. She was a better 'truth teller' than my well-meaning grandfather, who was impressed with status and celebrity, where he could show me off to his friends. I am a life member of his Avoca (Central Coast NSW) lawn bowls club. I have the badge to prove it. One day I will see if it still works at the club.

~ Eight ~

PLANNING NOW WHILE TRAINING

S etting up support systems while an athlete

Even though I wanted to play trains with my grandfather and desired to have a different relationship with him than we ended up having via his joy in collecting newspaper clippings, I valued his interest in me. It's challenging to predict the kind of social and emotional support you'll need after you stop playing sports because everyone's circumstances are different, including how you've learned to cope with life. Did your parents shield you from adversity? Did they compensate for your mistakes or bad behaviour, or did they allow you to come up against life's' boundaries and deal with disappointments or discipline? If you enjoyed many acts of, 'I'll do it for you' your coping mechanisms may be lacking when you need them as a retiring adult athlete.

As well as the structure of your sport, many of your needs were taken care of by the system that supported your sports career. These are services you assumed would continue, many are invisible. Some of these are plane and hotel tickets booked, uniforms paid for, entries created, records submitted for verification, event appearances scheduled, training plans devised, medical recovery sessions offered, and club rooms maintained. Normal daily routines are assumed too.

The structured schedules of my swimming routines meant I didn't have to do the hard work of planning my days or find other meaningful activities. I just had to be personally organised to do the training I liked to do. I had parents, sisters, coaches and officials taking care of my sport needs. It was a service to me with minimal reward for them.

If you've read the previous chapters and done some of the optional written tasks, you will have a list of the things people do for you just because you're an athlete. By analysing this realistically, you can identify which privileges may no longer be available once you retire. You may be offended and surprised.

The words to the chorus of the song Big Yellow Taxi sung by Joni Mitchell say it most fittingly.

"Don't it always seem to go
That you don't know what you got 'til it's gone…"

It is crucial to prepare, learn, and understand the sports career transition process to be ready for the inevitable changes after you stop playing sports. There is a good life awaiting you.

In the back of this book, I've listed some websites where you can get help or further understanding of Sports Career Transition. One is www.athletecareertransition.com with international reach. Another for Australians is https://anytimecounselling.com.au/counselling-for-ex-athletes/

Academic research has demonstrated that while problems of athletes retiring is well known to occur, what to do about it is less understood.

There are some limitations of the existing athlete career transition programs provided for elite athletes, but they may be worth having a look at and doing if they are offered by your organisation. As I've alluded to or described already, there are preventive measures that can be acted on yourself. That is the beauty of this book, providing possible precautionary measures. The reason is to reduce the worst possible effects of a difficult sports career transition. As I've already stated, an athlete in transition can experience grief from loss, an emotion that can be hard to deal with.

Grief from the loss of your usual life can appear in unexpected ways. Knowing that it takes time to process losses is a good start. It takes time to evolve and adapt to change too. According to Elizabeth Kubler-Ross who described phases of grief, Anger and Blaming can come about. Having someone in the know like a counsellor to talk to will defuse or help to process these feelings. You can blame the system, the coach, a fellow player for being dropped from the team. You can be angry at yourself for not applying yourself more or be angry with the neighbour's dog for barking when you need to sleep. A word of advice speaking in my mother's voice, even when you're unsettled, angry or sad, try maintaining good manners.

Having a broad understanding of how a career transition occurs can be helpful. This book is one resource. Check out some websites listed in the back for stories and helps in UK, Canada, USA and Australia. Hearing stories from other athletes can be lessons you can learn from. You are not alone in facing the reality of leaving your sport behind and embarking on a new journey in life, aiming to adapt to new ways of living. Even though you hear other people's stories of how they have transitioned away from their sport, your own journey will be unique.

Try not to judge yourself in comparison with another person's journey.

You might be at a stage in your transition where you need to know how to get a job, so that becomes your focus of attention in someone else's story. My current interest in reading other people's Sports Career Transition story is how they make meaning of their experience, perhaps an uplifting story or a saying that they share.

Returning to the topic of this chapter Setting Up Support, the most important support in a career transition comes from the people who care about you. These are the individuals who offer honest feedback rather than just saying yes to everything. Cultivating genuine and trustworthy relationships with these "truth tellers" is an investment in yourself and your support network.

The second biggest help is talking and telling stories about the ups and downs of your sports life, including challenges, fears, struggles, glories, self-doubt, celebrations, and training fatigue – the entire range of experiences of being a top-level athlete. One avenue might be speaking at schools as a guest to encourage those young people to be active or to challenge themselves in some endeavour. Addressing adult groups can be opportunities to share your story to help make sense of it while discovering 'life lessons' from the telling.

Recently, I was at a school in Tasmania speaking to students aged 10-12 about the Paris 2024 Olympics, the Olympic Games in general, and my interesting life. A girl asked how she might be able to tell her parents and friends that she doesn't want to play a particular sport anymore. I gave a general response about it being okay to want to do something different, but I also emphasized the importance of ensuring that she had something else to do to fill the time. Crucially, I advised her to finish out the season she had originally committed to, before making her final decision. I suggested that she talk it over with her parents and friends, while also keeping her options open. I re-emphasized that she should make sure she did some other activity, look forward to something else, not just stop doing the thing she no longer enjoys.

Children playing recreational youth sports can have similar dilemmas as elite athletes!

Imagination is a useful planning tool to work on with your support people. While you are still competing you can imagine what your future could look like. Then you can plan for it. Imagining the future is creating the future. What a persuasive expression! Thought experiments are another way of describing and imagining the future. Think it through without doing it yet. Once you have even a small picture in mind, you can start designing the necessary steps to transition away from your current sporting commitments and towards your new life. Below is a list of the kind of support you can establish before you depart from the structured assistance you've been accustomed to during your athletic career.

- Maintain trusted relationships, people you can talk to honestly without them judging your actions, but people from whom you will receive 'the truth'
- Psychological support - the team psychologist or a counsellor or professional confidant
- Think about what activity you would like to do and start looking for clubs or locations you can ease into before you quit. It might not be your 'final' activity, but it can be a bridge to discovering other ways to enjoy moving.
- Consider your family support and begin to ask them how you can contribute to their ambitions once you have time.
- Practise writing your retirement speech that you will give to your friends, your team, and your public fans.

- Other supports that are helpful to set up before you retire are friends with whom you can be authentic. New friends and new associates will be made because you will be mixing with other people.
- Embrace new opportunities with gusto. Refuse to accept that the best part of life has happened already.

Another way to prepare is to take more responsibility for your health/medical care. Sport can be physically demanding. It is rare that an athlete pushing their bodies to extreme capacities will not have some sort of strain injuries or serious pain from a playing or training injury. While you are engaged with the sport, the club or team will have medical personnel on hand to get you back to full playing potential as quickly as possible. The medics will have your measurements and note if the metrics are close to or far off your healthy baseline. Without the doctors, masseuses or the team psychologist, you can easily fall into a life of painful movement, or problematic blood issues like anaemia, bone density declines, heart muscle issues, and depressed moods. You need to take control of your own medical needs and understand what the measurements mean, like cholesterol, joint health, hydration, and blood pressure.

Ask around for what medical help is available to you through your club and how long after you are no longer playing, that help will continue. A caring club or players' association should understand this type of need for their retiring members. If not, you could ask that it be established.

Besides physical health check-ups, consider mental health checks. Mental health is a broad category of conditions. One definition of mental health is:

'a state of mental well-being that enables people to cope with the stresses of life, realize their abilities, learn well and work well, and contribute to their community'

A change in identity during retirement can affect mental health.

If you have played sport for 10 to 20 years your identity is tightly entwined with being an athlete. It may have become a *'one-dimensional'* identity with the no depth or breadth beyond the totalising/all-consuming sport environment. Coaches can become one-dimensional too with the same negative effects. After you retire you will still be who you have been as an athlete, but you will morph your identity by adding to it by doing other things in your life. You will become *multi-dimensional* over time. If you are a young person reading this it's a good idea for all adolescents to explore their identity, it is the time of life for that personal development to occur.

There is a concept called "identity foreclosure" which is observed in athletes who achieve a high level of success at a young age. This term refers to when the individual commits to a particular identity without exploring other options. Alternately it could be their parents or the people around them who consign the young person to a one-dimensional, closed identity. When a young athlete does the identity foreclosing, they may exhibit traits such as obedience, a strong need for approval, resistance to change, authoritarianism in parental styles, and conformity to conventional thinking.

I believe some resistance to my parents and the media stemmed from their imposition of a pre-determined identity on me. I sometimes felt stifled, as if I was frozen in time and unable to progress as I matured. I wanted to explore different personas, like any normal teenager. I experimented with a surfer chick look, adopted a hippy style and language, and wore a caftan and leather

"Jesus" sandals. That felt great to me, but it confused some adults in my life especially my father who had trouble with 'retiring' from being the father of Shane Gould the swimmer. He gained a lot of kudos in his workplace. His marketing roles emphasised the significance of being a famous father. Sadly, he struggled to accept a lot of my values, choices, and lifestyles right up until he died in 2017 when he was nearly 90. When he developed vascular dementia, he would refer to Princess Shane, of past glories. It was a clash to my outlook because I don't like living in the past. It also prevented me from relating to him adult to adult.

Over the years, particularly when I was young, I would sometimes find myself in confusion about my identity, because the Shane Gould one-dimensional swimmer-recognition was so dominant. I would say to myself or write on a piece of paper, "Would the real Shane please stand up!" Eventually, I accepted that all the different identities I lived out were meshed.

Humans can hold different roles, perform various jobs, and nurture assorted relationships while still being the same person. So, I can be a daughter, a wife, a friend, a mother, an auntie, a colleague, a teacher, each with different tasks to fulfill and interactions to perform, and I am still the same ME. Finding trusted people such as a counsellor can help identify the different identity roles you play.

If there is no-one you know well enough in your sport to talk about how you feel, you might be surprised about who turns up in your life on the 'other side' at just the right time that you need them, and they need you. Don't leave it to chance though. Be open to making close friendships, people you can share an interest with and develop authentic connections with. They might be someone who likes the same music, movies or books, or holiday locations as you do. Remember not to talk just about yourself. Everyone has a story, everyone has joys to share, and struggles to demystify. There are a lot of interesting people in your future world, but you won't know if you don't ask about them, then genuinely listen to what they say.

A further observation about medical support, especially to do with the adrenalin rush that competitions can provide. Please-please be aware if you have a tendency toward addictive behaviours to numb fatigue, bottled up emotional distress, anxiety causing poor sleep, or being unpractised to share feelings – drugs and alcohol can be tempting to use to self-medicate these situations. They do not help in the long run. There are 'oodles' of stories of great athletes being arrested for drunk and disorderly, gambling bankruptcy, driving under the influence, or associating with underworld figures dealing in illegal drugs.

This is not good for you, nor your reputation on which you might need to rely to get sponsorships, jobs, or to travel – some countries won't give a visa to a person with a criminal record. Get help before you retire if your truth-tellers notice this tendency to over-indulgence or a tendency to addiction. If you take pride in how many beers you can drink in an evening or on a long plane trip, I'd be worried for you. One rather famous Australian swimmer was an alcoholic. His friends arranged an intervention to get him help which worked for several years. But he was programmed from his early teenage years of success and celebrity to expect adulation, and entitlement, when he learned the practise of charm and the pleasures of fine food and wine. It was rather too late for him to have prepared for life without the addictive adulation he had grown up with and the substitute for adulation - alcohol.

~ Nine ~

PREPARATIONS AS YOU PLAN TO RETIRE

More preparations before you officially 'retire'

If you are not forced to retire by injury or other situations out of your control, making the decision to retire is probably one of the biggest decisions you will make in your life.

You must 'listen' to your gut instincts. You must weigh up your options and imagine a life without sport. Plan to live differently, which means change. Failing to plan for a life without sport can make your impending decision scary. Ultimately, it is your choice whether to leave or stay in it longer. You may already have a way of making big decisions, as life is full of them. However, the dilemma of stopping your sport can be agonizing.

When I had to make a life changing choice, I was in the country city of Armidale NSW where my parents had moved with my two younger sisters who were still in high school. It is a rural city surrounded by farmland, rolling rocky hills and forests. It gets cold being high in altitude, even early in summer. I had to make a choice to sign a commercial contract or not. I read the contract offered me by Arena, my dad explained the legal fine print and my mother asked meaningful questions. I couldn't make the final decision. I had to get away to a place of solace to think and feel my way through the difficult situation. I drove out of the Armidale urban areas along a quiet country road. I stopped beside a bridge spanning a small shallow stream, flowing over rocks and through deeper pools. Without much hesitation, I wandered down to the water, stripped naked and lay down in the cold flowing water, looking up at the sunny sky. I basked in that place with the chilly water tickling my shoulder and legs, my back bumping sometimes on the smooth warm rocks, at peace with the decision I had already made. I just had to sign the contract. In that moment I knew it was water I loved, being a swimmer, moving, working with it, being held, and squeezed by its flows pressure and buoyancy. I was only stopping the competitive part of swimming; I could still enjoy being in water. Reanimated by the stream, I clambered out, got dressed and drove home to my future life. I was ready for it, had family support and a rough plan about what to do next. As in planning for all futures, there are unknowns that can be a surprise. That's another story.

I've already suggested some things to do in the previous chapter – setting up systems with some specific ideas – before you retire. Let's now go through some more specific items that could be done as a sort of workbook, a guide to tasks that you can work on before you officially retire. Over the years I created lists of tasks. I like lists, they look so good crossed through or ticked off!

Here is a review of what to expect to occur when you transition from your sport career to your career after sport. Let's divide the jobs into nine areas of preparation.

Medical what is your local GP's phone number? Where can you get a massage? Have your medical records sent to a new GP if you move to another town

Emotional Attend to your feelings, your hopes, your memories, your friends

Physical Find a new way to move

Education this includes work experience, on the job training and formal study.

Challenges some goal to set which is challenging and you need to develop or hone skills for something creative or to accomplish.

Service Consider volunteering, being the helper not the receiver of help

Lists of what Im good at – soft skills, transferable skills

Create a food diary – jot down everything you eat and drink during a whole week and when you consume it. This is a 'tell' providing evidence of your eating habits and food quantities. The food diary makes unconscious habits conscious. The data is useful for yourself or for a dietician if you need help from a professional.

Question for consideration – what do people do for me because I am an athlete that probably won't be done after I retire?

Even if you're not a diarist or able to write out your feelings, just do as many of the suggested tasks as possible. Come back to them a few days later and add more insight. It's for your benefit or to share with a doctor or counsellor.

Next, implement the easiest action first that looks the most enjoyable. Then try the hardest one. Go back and forward until you get the hang of the exercises and start to really understand in a practical way, what is involved in transitioning. It will help your imagination – what life post sport career may look like. It could alleviate some anxiety for your decision to retire if you are more in control of what you need to do and what you can look forward to.

After I stopped swimming training, I did a traineeship as a swimming teacher. The students were children who could swim in deep water but were ready to learn strokes. It was my first paid job, and I loved helping the kids become more competent. Seeing their little faces light up when they mastered a movement was a delight. It was a clever way for my coach to stay in touch with me, as it was his swim school. It also took me out of the self-preoccupation I was wallowing in. I also coached a netball team as a volunteer and did some umpiring for the local games.

Volunteering is a terrific way to serve others rather than being on the receiving end. I visited old-aged hospices and disabled children care centres when I worked with some paid sponsors in the 1970's. I still spend 10-20% of my time and income on charitable projects.

One of my relatives became redundant from work in his 50s. Because he had time, he volunteered at a suburban soup kitchen, which gave him a sense of purpose and time to adapt to not working for money. He met new people there before starting a part-time job in another industry. There are similarities between retiring from work and retiring from sport, especially if you are forced to retire.

Redundancy is a bitter pill to swallow. If you have a public speaking gig someone in your audience will identify with you when they hear your sport retirement story. You might be surprised by the connection you can make with others who have had a similar experience. Many workers have lost their jobs or junior athletes have been cut from the track team. You can commiserate together or just realise you are not alone in your unfortunate experience.

A further reminder about personal responsibility ;

If you have found yourself in situations where others have said, "I'll do it for you," it's time to take more responsibility for yourself. This means practising personal organisation skills such as compiling receipts, doing laundry, maintaining your car, paying bills, scheduling, and keeping appointments, cooking, and eating nutritious meals, budgeting, and managing money, planning meals, and keeping up with regular health checks and immunisations, as well as maintaining a clean-living space. These are all part of the natural process of growing up and becoming a responsible adult, so don't be too proud to learn these essential skills then do them.

Some other tips.

To keep track of appointments and time-sensitive meetings, using an alarm and a keeping a calendar diary can be very helpful. Phone calendars can do both. Keep track of and conscious of your skills, no matter how small they may seem. Writing them down looks great as a long list on paper.

More life-skills for the list includes knowing how to operate a dishwasher, change a car tyre, write a thank you card, and send it. Building these skills can give you confidence, especially if you feel like you've been left behind by well-established friends in their jobs and lives. It's also a way to recognise the value of your time in sports, what it has taught you, and what you are capable of. This includes dealing with disappointment, handling success, setting, and achieving goals, and continually setting new goals and planning how to accomplish them.

I did set new goals for myself and developed new skills as part of my adaptation to my post sport life. I worked with international sports companies, surfed, became a sheep and horse farmer, and read widely. Staying in touch somehow with your sport colleagues and lifestyle is up to you. As I have said already, I had some contact with the swimming world and that identity through swimming lessons. I also did the occasional 'where are they now' interview.

~ Ten ~

MEMORY 'BANKING'

Memory banks, photos, video, interviews and writing or talking about your experience (whatever suits you best).

Post-sport life can become very busy with reorganising daily routines, attending courses, starting new challenges, fulfilling family commitments, and organising paperwork. I believe it is a great idea to make time to create memory banks to honour your sport life.

After relocating from Sydney to my new home in Margaret River, Western Australia, I was unsure what to do with my trophies, memorabilia, team uniforms, correspondence, medals, and certificates. As a temporary solution, I packed some of these items into four wooden tea chests and arranged for them to be shipped across the country once I had a mailing address. I left behind a beautiful oak cabinet at my parent's house, which my grandfather had repurposed to store my medals and certificates neatly. Later, my Olympic medals were housed in my own home before being exhibited at a sports museum in Perth. They were briefly displayed in Canberra at the Institute of Sport complex museum before finding a permanent home at the Australian Sports Museum in Melbourne on loan. I've lost track of some of my memorabilia, but some was donated to a museum in New South Wales and is now located within the Sydney 2000 Olympic Games precinct.

Like me, your sport life has been filled with memorable moments. Create a system for collecting and storing photographs, press clippings, speeches, and video posts. This will allow you to 'bank' your memories both literally and metaphorically. My computer files are full of written speeches, presentations and more recently digital photos and addresses of contacts made while doing projects or promotions.

Creating visual archives of your sports life can be beneficial for promoting yourself after your sports career. You can leverage your popularity while controlling how you present yourself to others, effectively curating your own biography. I have limited photographs and video of my sport life because they were analogue and owned by other people. Digital images are so much easier to own and store.

If you keep a logbook or diary, they can be great resources for storytelling and recalling details. I have three years of detailed logbooks that the NSW library bought in 1998. Along with Ned Kelly's helmet and Don Bradman's green cricket cap, they went on a national tour. They became nationally important historical documents appreciated by all who read them.

A form of 'talk therapy' is storytelling. Remember, it's important to talk about your experiences in sports to help make sense of them. Making meaning of situations, conversations, actions, objects, is part of making sense of your subjective experiences. Having conversations with someone who listens with empathy can be helpful to cross check with the meanings, accurate or inaccurate you have concluded.

It's also important to remember that others have also accomplished remarkable things, not just you. At some point, you may find it helpful to seek the support of a professional counsellor rather than depending on friends. Listen to those who care about you and may recognise when you need help before you realise it yourself. This book is not a substitute for professional support. There is no shame in getting help, you are not crazy. There are numerous things that have happened to you. It can be hard to untangle history, events and people. There is such a thing as historical fiction too. I relied on my mother and father to provide facts and their impressions when I wrote my autobiography in 1998.

One image I had of my life in sport is a pot of vegetable soup. It's hard to distinguish the peas from the broccoli, the carrot from the pumpkin – metaphors for the varied episodes and people in your life. Taking the metaphor further a pot of vegie soup is very nourishing and tasty. Your life in sport has many positives.

~ Eleven ~

GRATITUDE AND AFFIRMATIONS

Celebrations and affirmations, anniversaries, and gratitude

How do you celebrate your achievements? It's a personal thing. Everyone has their own way of commemorating their accomplishments. I don't think I celebrated enough after winning records and medals. There were so many of them. I was young too, which limited the number of ways to celebrate. Winning them was not the only point to me, though, which confused my sensibilities. I discovered later that making meaning of my medals and records was of greater significance than recognition. Receiving instruction to improve is one meaning. Another is appreciating the joint humanity of people around the world just wanting to develop their talents, do meaningful work and love and be loved. Travelling to competitions gave me those perspectives.

A life in sport is worth acknowledging through some sort of ritual, public or private. Even though your life in sport may be over, feel confident about celebrating your accomplishments that provide meaning and life satisfaction.

A thought about accomplishments. I think there's a distinction between accomplishments and achievements. "Accomplish" encompasses all the skills you brought into play for your sports career. The things you did to become a good athlete. Dedication and trying hard come to mind. An "achievement" is the outcome of what you obtained. I appreciate this difference. Word meanings are valuable when used correctly. I recall the different values I have, it's the intrinsic values that sustain my memories rather than the extrinsic rewards. A regular question I get is 'What does it feel like to stand on the podium with your medal?' What I recall is the pleasure of trying hard, the joy of moving in the water, the thrill of racing someone better than me, and the satisfaction of improving my times. The medal and the ceremony are symbols of all the intrinsic values, not the main 'Thing'. I do love to compete too. I see it as a coming together to mutually help each other to perform best as you can on the day – because of your competitor who pushes you to extraordinary effort.

Celebrations are an individual choice, which can take on a variety of forms, traditional or quirky. Right after the Olympics, I attended the closing ceremony much to the concern of my parents. Because I had done well winning 5 individual medals, they thought that Palestinian terrorists who murdered Israeli athletes might do another attack on athletes, especially Mark Spitz who was Jewish. They didn't attack again, and I was amongst the jumble of athletes who celebrated the end of the Games in the closing ceremony.

However, as I've already narrated, there was no ticker tape reception back in Australia, except at my school, Turramurra High School. It seems that Australian officials, the government, and the AOC were unsure whether to mourn the Israeli deaths or celebrate the Australian team. I won 20% of Australia's medals that year, with three golds, one silver, and one bronze. A big public reception would have completed my Olympic 'project'.

The trophy room is a popular way to remember, but be careful of it becoming a shrine, holding you back in the past. Im not a trophy room person, but I did have some cabinets with drawers that my mother carefully arranged medals and ribbons. She laid them out in chronological order, from the first medal I won and the time I did it in, through the seven years of events I competed in, to the penultimate Olympic Medals in their five boxes in the bigger bottom drawer. Poppa Reid who made the scrapbooks, also made the medal cabinet out of an oak bedside table.

Putting my medals on the church altar at the Gordon Methodist church in Sydney within a month of returning from Munich was an unconventional but appropriate way for me to celebrate. My mother's research on the ancient Olympians' placing their laurel wreaths on the altar of their hometown guided me. The purpose for the Ancient Olympians was to thank the gods for their success.

Club fundraising events and being honoured by sports organizations with sportswoman of the year awards are all great affirmations of your achievements in your sports career. Some well-loved individuals have had facilities named after them and receive these honours as a celebration of their accomplishments.

About 14 years after I 'retired' I received an MBE, a Queens honour – Australia is still under British influence as a constitutional monarchy. I attended a fancy function in Perth government house, a garden party where I was presented with the award by Queen Elizabeth. My husband and two of my children attended too, so I could share that with them. It was all rather posh and felt out of place dressed up in a borrowed dress and hat, but I gloated in the attention with my husband witnessing it.

Anniversaries of championship wins, and honours bestowed, affirm the value of your life in sport. There is a danger, though. Ruminating on what could have been, can be detrimental to adjusting to your new life. 'Living in the past' doesn't help your present or future life either.

I recall at least two 1972 Olympic team reunions fondly. At those events, I learned more about my teammates' life journeys, struggles, joys, disappointments, in reflection to my own experiences. Most of us had lived ordinary lives with the background of extraordinary experiences of our Olympian swimming life.

My swimming club Ryde and my coach Carlile's organisation have invited me over the years to attend events to honour swimmers and coaches and raise money for their foundation. I do believe because of my youth 14-17 at the top of my sport, I did not form strong bonds with my training mates and travel teammates. It didn't help that I left the East Coast where many celebratory events were held, to live on the other side of the country in Western Australia. Circumstances like those can inhibit the feeling of belonging and group celebrations and honours.

Over the years, the adulation felt like too much. I felt it froze me in the past as a sweet 15-year-old girl. However, as my parents taught me, receive awards graciously, be polite to autograph hunters and the media.

'Where are they now?' type stories in magazines and TV documentaries can be helpful to be honoured with. I also got paid sometimes, which funded our annual family camping holiday in wild places on wild coasts!

Honour. Honour is an interesting word with varied meanings. The Bible says to honour your mother and father, meaning respect and possibly obey. The honour roll board at school or sports club is a sign for achievements higher than others. It helps another generation to know the history of their sport too.

Honour your talents means don't squander them, respect them to use them wisely and with gratitude (to your parents or the gift from a higher power if you believe in one). Honour your intuition, and your special athletic know-how that helped you become a top-level athlete. Honouring your coach and teammates would be like honouring parents. Somewhere in there is being honoured yourself by other people.

I value the characteristic of humility, so I practise that. Being gracious is a way of expressing gratitude. You can be proud standing tall to accept awards and honours for being the champion. Let your athleticism, clever game strategy, your sportsmanship speak for you. Avoid boasting about the obvious – you're good at what you do/did. At the same time 'don't hide your light under a basket' is a biblical saying. Self-respecting pride not arrogant pride.

Transferable skills

Grab hold of all the identified features that made you good and bring them across to your different life without sport. These are the *transferable skills*. Keep adding to the list if something more comes to mind. You might realise how you are good at resolving arguments between players, write that down. You might recall how kids loved to get your autograph first. What is your personality that you exude that causes children to be drawn to you? That trait may be a good indication that you could work in youth sports to encourage and teach the next generation of sportspersons.

The next piece of advice that I think will be useful is to continually identify the soft (life) skills sport has given you. This can also be an affirmation to you while helping you to encourage children to play sport, not just for the physical and competition. Soft skills are a recent concept since they have been recognised in business. Resolving team conflict, and work ethic are soft skills whereas hard skills are the technical ones such as operating machinery or devices.

More recently there is a recognition of types of labour that is mostly undertaken by women in a family. Intellectual labour, planning labour, the cognitive load thinking about all the practical elements of household responsibilities, such as shopping, meal planning and preparation, organising playdates, and birthday presents.

Emotional labour is more often taken care of by women to maintain the family's emotions, calming things down if kids act up. Worrying about how they are coping at school. The mental load involves preparing, organising, and anticipating everything emotional and practical that needs to get done to make life flow. Male athletes need to watch particularly for this entitlement they have been socialised to expect, while women athletes need to be sure they are confident enough to speak openly with a partner to discuss sharing this labour, some of the 'soft skills' life load.

I found myself revelling in the responsibilities of wife-mother-farmer-joint-income earner. During the intensity of parental responsibilities of a brood of young children I was proud of and glad I had the experience of pacing myself in long distance events and hard training sessions. Making it to the children's bedtime was an endurance event. I got over the pride of that idea when I had my fourth baby. I had to ask my parents for help. I had pride in my physicality and the emotional and planning labour I took on. My mother and father moved from one side of the country to the other, saying 'Shane, this is the first time we recall that you have asked for help. We knew you needed it, so we had to respond.' Motherhood was another enjoyable physical challenge I could revel in until I couldn't do it without help.

I discovered that much of the household labour is invisible and hard to measure or know when it starts and when it ends. Living on a dusty farm, meant dirt was traipsed into the house requiring a sweeping up to 5 times a day. I loved making piles of dirt to scoop up with a dustpan and brush. A 'shoe pile' outside the kitchen door reduced the sweeping to 2 to 3 times a day. Quite a different satisfaction to achieving training set times and winning races.

Similarly, the soft skills learned in sports are hard to measure because they are not typically recognised as normalised work or skills.

Because I hadn't reconciled my swimming career with my life without competition, training, accolades, and the excitement of physical effort, and was in philosophical conflict about the nature of competition, I vacillated between love and hate for this powerful identity Shane Gould the swimmer and all the of the structures supporting it. Retiring was both a relief from the obligations and yet I missed the lifestyle. After I debriefed and over time, I reconciled my personas into one coherent individual who grasped the meaning of swimming, its extra associated happenings, pleasures, and learnings. Some of which have been described in my stories.

I now know that I don't have to 'get over' the sense of loss or have any finality of acceptance or concluding resolution. The pain of the 'living loss' of sport relationships doesn't go away, it just becomes more manageable with time and support.

When I felt burdened by the weight of loss or feeling guilty about being relieved when I was no longer competing/performing, I had feelings of being ambivalent about the value of anyone participating in organised sport. Strange what unresolved grief can make you think. I believe some forms of sport are a great value especially well-run youth sport based on participation and life lesson values. When I did a PhD study of swimming culture the research involved observing and interviewing people connected with age group swimming clubs and teachers conducting drowning prevention lessons. Good research can challenge preconceived notions and attitudes. One research interview changed my attitude toward the value of age group swimming.

Affirming the value of swimming skills altered my perspectives

Research is a way of testing your ideas and beliefs, needing to be open to have them disputed, even disproved. My subject *The Culture of Swimming,* was about what swimming meant to Australians, how it was practised and organised. Competition swimming was a small but important part of the study. One aspect of my PhD was reviewing competition swimming memberships, the numbers of clubs, the redundancies (families who didn't re-enrol). I travelled in 2016 with my husband Milt as co-driver across southern Australia for 10 weeks in a motor home to observe swimming pools, river, and sea swimming, talk to pool managers, beach and river users, swimming club parents, adult bathers, and masters' swimmers. In the remote city of Broken Hill, a mining town in the outback, I spoke with volunteer coaches at a swimming club. They convinced me of the importance of country swimming clubs to be inclusive of kids who would never be champions but loved the activity and the social engagements. This changed my attitude about encouraging children to join swimming clubs and my perspective of being a junior competitor before I entered the top levels of the sport.

I recalled my enjoyment of Saturday races, handicap events, ice cream after the club barbecue, racing around on the grass, bouncing on trampolines, or daring to jump off the high diving platform. I first met a person with a disability at the Ryde club, a young man with Down syndrome, the brother of Gail Neall the other Olympic champion at my high school. Gail's brother was welcomed to race with others and often won the timed handicap 50 metres when the faster swimmers had to chase him down the pool.

As I listened to the Broken Hill swim club coach telling me about her values for the club, I remembered my experiences enjoying being in a swimming club. The Broken Hill club members were excitedly planning fundraising events to attend the annual

3day interclub competition in Mildura 300km away. A significant travel trip for the country kids to go away, camp and compete in another town.

The volunteers I spoke to during my research also reminded me that youth sport needs people to generously give up their time to enable events to be conducted. Fortunately, my parents trained me when I was young to thank the timekeepers, the judges, and the starters for giving kids a chance to be competitively active. The officials often stood in cold winds and drizzly rain or hot sun. Their volunteering helped young people learn the way-of-an-athlete.

Being involved with sports has many benefits, both hard and soft skills. This is an affirmation to me and to you that our time in sport is worth it, even though you may be feeling otherwise right now. Gratitude is a cure for entitlement. Gratitude will help you connect with people you can trust. Gratitude is a passport to new opportunity.

Back to you as a person adapting to life after sport. By volunteering at a school or at your local sports club, humility might generate more gratitude in yourself toward those people who helped you. When you experience what is involved with giving kids a chance to learn competition graces, about the capacity of their bodies, feeling OK about getting puffed, learning about the processes of improving through training and knowing and enjoying trying hard while respecting their competitors. Practising an attitude of gratitude toward the people, the culture, and the nation you have been helped by to achieve your best level of sport can help you transition to a new life of not receiving all the attention.

Being a standout athlete can make you feel uniquely important. The opportunities you've had are because of your talent and hard work. Your success is also because of your country's culture valuing sport. By being humble, not a 'spoiled brat' you're much more likely to adapt to another career. To live the inspiring, fulfilling life you want.

I hope that my stories have been an example of hope and struggle and the reward for systematically managing the transition for life after sport, even if you and I make mistakes along the way.

Work on the process and make the adjustments required. You now understand how to navigate your sports career transition with optimism with people you trust to help make sense of your life in sports and welcome the new different life to come.

Dr Shane Gould is a world champion swimmer, an Australian sporting legend. She has a PhD in the Culture of Swimming in Australia. She uses her personal career transition experiences and academic insights, to provide fresh understanding of the growing problem of athletes having difficulty adjusting mentally and emotionally to their life after sport.

AUTHOR DR SHANE GOULD
AUSTRALIAN SPORTING LEGEND

There is a high incidence of distress in retiring athletes but very little guidance to understand why and what to do about it. Athletes their families and coaches need this book as a Sports Career Transition guide. It will help top level athletes, district and college level players and may also assist young people who quit youth sport. Whether withdrawing by choice, dropped from a league team, or forced by injury, or having unrealistic goals, you need to understand the transition phase of your sporting life. Emotional and mental suffering after retirement is caused by a sense of loss, grief that feels like a bereavement. The grief is a non-death loss though. Loss of relationships, cheering crowds, loss of purpose, reduced physical exhilaration. Retiring from sport is an opportunity to begin another fulfilling life. The uncertain future can be scary. It may take months and years of adaptation, everyone is different. Having support is important.

Causes of problematic retirement
Well meaning people *I'll do it for you* who restrict independence.
A sense of entitlement
Feeling like you don't deserve success
Being treated as if you have 'special needs

Preparing before the final whistle while still training and competing
Expect some sort of grief from loss, what you will miss
Develop relationships with people you can trust
Stop expecting privileges however deserving you feel
Create alternatives to your team or squad camaraderie
Identify Transferable skills and Continue to stay active
Take care of other people's needs not just your own goals
Celebrate accomplishments with gratitude

Life after sport is a positive time for growth and development.

Suggested sources of help

https://olympics.com/athlete365/topics/career-plus
https://griefline.org.au/
https://www.betterhealth.vic.gov.au/conditionsandtreatments/mental-health-and-wellbeing
https://www.beyondblue.org.au/get-support
https://teamcanada.abiliticbt.com/en-CA
Canada Finding Yourself after Sport https://www.shootingstarpsychology.com/sport/
Wylleman P, Alfermann D & Lavallee D (2004) Career transitions in sport: European perspectives, Psychology of Sport and Exercise, 5 (1), pp. 7-20.
Career and Life Transitions https://www.blokespsychology.com.au/support/career-life-transition
https://careerahead.com.au/career-changers/athletes/
https://www.ais.gov.au/career-and-education/cprn
https://www.ais.gov.au/career-and-education/beyond-the-games
https://anytimecounselling.com.au/counselling-for-ex-athletes/
LIFELINE – crisis counselling 13 11 14 https://www.lifeline.org.au/about/our-services/
Player Support Services UK https://player-support.com/our-story/
Athletes Soul USA https://player-support.com/our-story/
USA https://counseling.northwestern.edu/blog/supporting-athletes-transitioning-out-of-sports/
Article UK Gordon, S., & Lavallee, D. (2012). Career transitions. In T. Morris & P. Terry (Eds.), The new sport and exercise psychology companion (pp. 567-582). Morgantown, WV: Fitness Information Technology.
Ernst and Young UK https://www.ey.com/en_gl/athlete-program
Australian Athletics https://www.athletics.com.au/high-performance/athlete-wellbeing-engagement
AFL Players Association https://www.aflplayers.com.au/news-feed/stories/you-need-to-take-this-opportunity-dont-waste-it
WALES https://www.athletecareertransition.com/

ACKNOWLEDGEMENTS

To Shirley Gould who taught me the difference between intrinsic motivations and extrinsic rewards. Also to Neil Innes who had to put up with the mess I made of my swimming career transition while we were married. Then to husband Milt Nelms who affirmed my talent and success freeing us up to work together to help people thrive in my post sports careers.